Sh

It

to know you -
sharing experiences.
Spread the word —
we need to protect
our children better.

The Best —
Jamie

God Bless the children!
Janie
2009

Angels Are Watching

By
J.D. Berger

authorHOUSE™

1663 LIBERTY DRIVE, SUITE 200
BLOOMINGTON, INDIANA 47403
(800) 839-8640
WWW.AUTHORHOUSE.COM

First published by AuthorHouse 06/03/05

ISBN: 1-4208-6234-0 (e)
ISBN: 1-4208-2691-3 (sc)

Printed in the United States of America
Bloomington, Indiana

This book is printed on acid-free paper.

AUTHOR'S NOTE

This is a story of a human tragedy. A young girl is on her way to womanhood. A young man who has lost his way.

By the end of writing this book, it finally struck me why I felt so compelled to tell this story. I wanted to make a statement about our children. We, as adults need to work much harder to nurture and protect them. But most of all, to set good examples of what a person of good character should strive to be. We need to put time into getting to know ourselves. We need to work on our own "issues" so that we can help to enrich our children's lives. We need to appreciate childbirth, not only as our God-given right, but also as our responsibility.

Between the years of 1980-1996, suicide increased in ten to fourteen year olds by 120%. Every seventy-eight seconds, a teen will attempt suicide. Every ninety seconds they will succeed. More teens smoke marijuana than do tobacco. Today 202 school children will be arrested for drugs. This year 5,315 teens will be arrested for a crime. Before the end of the day 3,506 children will have ran away from home. Ninety percent of all gang members are juveniles. Every twenty-four hours, 15,000 will try drugs for the first time. 2,795 girls will become pregnant. Every hour of every day a young person will contract HIV. Before the end of the school day 5,703 children will be the victims of a violent crime. In Los Angeles County child abuse cases are so prevalent that the average sentence may be only six months in prison. Probably because the legal system is so over-loaded. This is absurd! Who is looking out for our children?

While working as a counselor at the Ventura Youth Correctional Facility, every day I witness the impact of emotional neglect and abuse that our young people have endured. It takes many years to repair the damage to their souls, if ever.

WE CAN DO BETTER. OUR FUTURE DEPENDS ON IT!

This story is told from my own perspective and observations as a juror on this trial. There is no intention on my part to misrepresent the facts or statements made by persons involved in this case. In an effort to preserve the privacy and dignity of the sexual assault victims, I have changed their names. I believe that all involved in this story deserve some compassion, including the defendant, Vincent Sanchez.

LIFE IS PRECIOUS. DON'T WASTE YOURS! MAY THE ANGELS BLESS AND KEEP EACH AND EVERYONE THAT THIS STORY TOUCHES.

IN HONOR OF MEGAN

Do not stand at my grave and weep
I am not there, I do not sleep.
I am a thousand winds that blow
I am the diamond glint on snow.
I am the sunlight on ripened grain
I am the gentle rain,
when you wake in morning hush.
I am the swift uplifting rush of quiet
birds in circling flight.
I am the soft starlight at night.
Do not stand at my grave and weep
I am not there, I do not sleep.

Author unknown

Megan is in my thoughts this beautiful July fourth, two years following her death.

As we are listening to decide the fate of her killer, her family still grieves their loss. It is witnessed by the anguished look on her father's face. He does not smile or laugh. He does not appear to be the same person I knew five years ago. This won't be just another holiday to them, I'm sure. Probably they will never view July fourth the same way. This was the last day of Megan's life on earth. I hope that we, as the jury in this case, can help to bring closure to their pain. God bless the family of Megan Barroso, as I know he has blessed the spirit of Megan. Her spirit lives on in all the people who knew and loved her. I dedicate this book in her memory.

Alternate Juror #5
July 4, 2003

DAY ONE

I am number five alternate juror, taken from a pool of 800 people. I was the last and final person to be questioned. It only took a few minutes, and a barrage of questions, for both sides to say, "We will accept this juror, your honor."

Who knows what the attorneys really see in the faces of potential jurors. Why they keep some and why they let so many others go. We knew we were in for the long haul. The judge made sure we understood that. No financial burdens? No surgery planned or major health issues? No extended vacations, already paid for? No extreme views about rape, kidnap, and murder? "How do you feel about the death penalty?" both sides asked. But what about any mitigating circumstances, the Defense wants to know? Can you be fair and impartial? Are you prejudice against hispanics? How do you feel about our criminal justice system? Have you ever been victimized by anybody? Is there any of us alive on the planet who has not been victimized by someone, I wondered. These questions came after we had already filled out a thirty-page questionnaire with many of the same questions on it. And so it began.

I told my supervisors that I would be putting my job on hold for several months, maybe four. They accepted it much more cheerfully than I had expected. Almost as if they were cheering for me, and also hoping it could have been them who got pulled away for an "extended vacation," as they put it. If only it would feel like that in reality. What details would we jurors be exposed to? Could we really hold up under the stress of these heinous details? Afterall, we knew already that a young girl had possibly been kidnapped and raped. Later, she was killed. We learned this from the jury questionnaire.

There may be videotapes to watch, and painful stuff to hear. This Sanchez guy, the accused, was also the guy who was known as the "Simi Valley Rapist." This has all the makings of a horror movie! But unfortunately, living in our times have prepared us for horrible events. Can you talk about these details, sexual details with complete strangers? All the jurors believe they can. Is that because we have been repeatedly exposed to so many ugly images in movies, television, in books, and in our newspapers? What has happened to us as a society? "We have lost our souls." That is what Deepak Chopra says, and I agree. And we will judge a man who has lost his soul. Maybe even his life.

GETTING STARTED

Anticipation makes the first day exciting. This will be something completely new for all of us to ponder. New to me especially, because being alternate juror number five means that I may sit through this whole trial and maybe sentencing too, and not be allowed to make my opinions known. I give my opinions everyday in my work and many times a day. Keeping my mouth shut may be the hardest thing I ever have to do. But I welcome the challenge. To sit back, observe people and listen. I view this as a growth exercise for me. I also plan to journal my thoughts, so as to have a sounding board of sorts.

Getting to know the fellow jurors will be chapter one, I suppose. We have started to exercise our ability to work together by planning who will bring coffee, pot, cups, and such the first day. One man, number seven juror put in a request for homemade cookies.

The bailiff has warned us that the news media will try to corner us and ask questions. He has already given us some evasive techniques to use. Come to floor number two and he will take us up the back way to the fourth floor. Park in the far lot. It will be easier to get through the metal detectors on that side and the press will likely be waiting on the other side of the building.

Opening statements will be the first order of the day, Monday morning at nine o'clock.

OPENING STATEMENTS

Vincent Henry Sanchez, known as the "Simi Valley Rapist" is in the courtroom from the beginning of jury selection. He is a small, stocky man with dark brown hair and dark eyes. Sanchez does not resemble the monster that would be described to us in the opening statements and through victim's stories. He sits next to his lawyers and acts as if he has a great deal of work to do. I never see him look up or make any eye contact with anyone. Instead, he busies himself with paperwork. Who knows what he is recording but he stays busy, nonetheless.

He has already pleaded guilty to numerous counts of rape, kidnap, and great bodily harm. I believe there are twelve young ladies whose lives he touched. Thirteen, when you count Megan, however, he touched her life in a whole different way. He took it. The Defense told us this at the beginning of their opening statement. So, we will not be deciding his guilt about killing Megan, but if that was his intent. Also, in the process, if he intended to rape and/or kidnap her. These issues would also be deciding factors in whether or not he is eligible for the death penalty.

In the opening statements, the Prosecution went into great detail about his "confessed" crimes against his sexual victims. Prosecution statements lasted most of the day. I began to wonder why we needed all of the witnesses that were waiting to tell their story. After witnessing evidence and testimony about all the damage he has done, we only have to decide if he intended to rape or kidnap Megan in the process of killing her. This case is all about Sanchez' intentions toward Megan Barroso.

The Defense says it is a matter of circumstances. A matter of Sanchez' character. "Mr. Sanchez has more than one problem," the Defense stated. That sure is an understatement! He stalked woman. He peeped in their windows, and videotaped them undressing. He stole their possessions, especially their undergarments. He broke into their homes, threatening their lives and the lives of their family and pets if they did not cooperate, holding a knife to their throat. He sodomized several and made them orally copulate him. He videotaped his sexual assaults on them. He covered their heads with pillowslips, jackets or blankets. He raped them, sometimes repeatedly. Even stabbed one with a knife. He beat them if they resisted, and took their belongings as souvenirs. But it was different with Megan. He took her life and threw her body in a ravine. When she was found a month later, time and animals had desecrated much of her body. Most of the evidence surrounding what happened before her death was destroyed. The forensic experts would have to reconstruct the facts. But could they? Could anyone supply the bottom line? Why?

COLLEGE BOY?

Only five days after Sanchez dumped the body of Megan Barroso, he attacked his thirteenth victim. He had to pay for his actions, but how? That was another question we as the jury had to decide. Does he deserve the death penalty, or just life in prison? We, the public, have many thoughts on this subject. Should we have to pay for his care for the rest of his life with our tax dollars? Should he be able to have life without the possibility of parole, when he took Megan's? Could life in prison be stronger punishment than putting him to death? Should he pay the ultimate price—a life for a life? The families of the victims would probably say, "an eye for an eye." But whether the jurors would decide the death penalty, was the main focus of this case. The serious impact of this case on the families of the victims and the family of the defendant would weigh heavy on the minds of us having to decide his fate.

Sanchez was dressed in a shirt and tie, looking like a college boy. I wondered if he really dressed anything like that, or had the defense bought him this wardrobe. He sure did not have the charisma or confidence of a guy like O.J. He kept his head down. The only time I recall him even changing his demeanor was when the People played a taped phone call from his girlfriend of three years, Luz LaFarga. She had agreed to help the police by making a "cold call" to Sanchez and try to get him to say something about Megan, while the police recorded the call. This was when the search parties were still trying to find her body. From the bullet holes and blood in her car, investigators surmised that Megan had been wounded. Sanchez paused from his writing, as he listened intently to the words of Luz on the taped recording. He may have been listening even more intently on his own responses to her questions. He told Luz, He knew nothing and that "the cops are just trying to pin anything and everything on me." He also minimized his own involvement in the other confessed crimes, changing his story for his girlfriend to, "Only five, not eleven assaults." As if raping, sodomizing, hurting, degrading only five women was not as bad as eleven! One of the young girls was believed to be a fifteen-year-old virgin. What kind of person would do this to another human being? I am almost sure by the end of the four months, we will know what kind of person Vincent Sanchez really is.

LIFE FOR THE LIVING

How does one quiet the mind? Nobody told us that we would have these images and thoughts running around in our heads for days afterwards. I began to fear for my own safety. After hearing how he stalked these young woman, I started paying particular attention to the locking of my own doors and securing my windows.

The night after opening statements, I woke up around three-fifty. Finally, I got up and made a cup of hot chocolate before falling back to sleep. I rehearsed in my mind how I would get to the gun that my husband had left in the nightstand, if I ever need to defend myself. I felt more comfortable just using my mace. I had experience with the use of mace, not with a gun.

My plan is to keep myself balanced. Exercise, listen to relaxing music, sing in the sunshine, enjoy my friends and family, take hot soothing baths, and be among the living.

The details just pop up in your mind at the strangest times. While looking at a blouse on the rack of T.J. Max, or watching kids cross the street. Life goes on for the living.

I wonder how it goes on for the parents of Megan? I knew Art and Susan Barroso from a previous job at Camarillo State Hospital. I made sure that the court knew this ahead of time. Both sides seemed to be okay with it. After all, I had not seen or talked to either of them in years. Maybe four or five years now. After the hospital closed, everyone who worked or lived there was displaced all over the state of California. I had heard that Art went to Fairview State Hospital. I was not sure what Susan was doing now. I knew they had divorced some years ago and moved to different towns. I never met Megan. I only knew she existed when she no longer existed.

I hoped the first day Art saw me in the jury box, it would give him some sort of comfort. I could not know his pain. However, I saw the shell that he walked around in.

FIGHTING FOR YOUR LIFE

The Prosecution's exhibit #1 is a large poster board with all of Sanchez' victims (at least the ones that are known), and the dates when they were victimized. In the past few days we have been putting real faces to these photographs. Even the photo faces seem to cry out for justice. Six of the assault victims have testified in the past two days. Luckily, the judge is able to keep the press away. Well, at least the photographers are kept at bay.

Most all of these young women tell a similar story. (Caught by surprise, forced, photographed in compromising positions, some injured pretty bad if they resisted him at all.) Annette, the tenth victim told a different story. She seemed to hold her own with Sanchez. She fought back, but had the injuries to show for it. She had bruises all over her face and body, bite mark on the thumb, cut in the middle of her back, and was hit four times in the head with a beer bottle, but no stitches. However, she did suffer some memory loss, disorientation, eye problems and back problems. One might think that she did

11

not come out of this episode in very good shape, but at least Sanchez did not rape her. For this reason, her injuries were downplayed when she went to the hospital for an assault exam. This seemed to upset her as much as the original assault. (She stated she was a spiritual person and felt that if she prayed, the negative energy would spare her.) I guess that is a matter of opinion. I remember thinking throughout her testimony, at least she was not raped or sodomized like most of the others. This by no means is meant to minimize her pain or injury. It appears from her testimony, that she may have suffered the most severe physical injury due to her resisting. The saying-- you never really know how you will react until you are in the situation-- applies here. I found myself applauding her for her attempts to, "save her own life." That is what she thought she was doing-- fighting for her life.

As I mentioned, Annette got her licks in too. She bite Sanchez, broke a wooden frame over his head, pulled him to the ground, covered his face with his own hooded sweatshirt, and slugged him back when he was attacking her with his fists. She got out of the plastic tie cables that he had placed on her ankles twice and the ones tying her hands together. Finally, she managed to get a chair between the two of them and threatened him with a metal lamp. Now, I wonder how long it took before he assaulted another female? It wasn't clear what <u>his</u> injuries were that night, but needless to say, I bet he did not report them.

Annette managed to keep her life and go on to receive a Doctorate in Chiropractic Medicine. She presents herself as a very strong and determined lady. She prayed at the end of her testimony, while the attorney's fought over which statements would be allowed into evidence. As she leaves the witness stand, she looked directly into my face and said,"thank you." As she walked away, I said a silence prayer for her, and all of the young women hurt by Sanchez. I hope that she felt it.

GOOD VERSES EVIL

I guess it may sound like I have already made up my mind regarding Sanchez' guilt. Well, I have. As a matter of fact, I have grown to despise this man. But, let me explain. The facts thus far, have already been substantiated by evidence, a Grand Jury Hearing, and Sanchez' own confessions. So, I was not jumping to conclusions without all the evidence. You may ask why then, are we having to listen to all of his past transgressions? Well, I felt the same way. But the Defense Attorney states that we will have to weigh these facts and attempt to see the patterns present and compare them to Megan's case and then draw a conclusion about Sanchez' intentions. The Defense has gone to great lengths to accomplish this, with several very detailed charts. Their goal is to prove ultimately, that the death of Megan Barroso did not fit Sanchez' usual pattern. His pattern of stalking, raping, photographing, and taking of the victim's possessions. This will be the cornerstone to the question of whether Sanchez should die for his crime against Megan Barroso. These repeated crimes against other young women would serve as aggravating circumstances.

Sanchez definitely had a method of operation. He almost always stalked and photographed his potential victims. He wore dark clothing, sweatshirt, ski mask, dark gloves and jogging shoes. He usually came in through a window. He acted as if he cared about the well being of these women while he was taking their spirit and threatening their lives. He even inquired on many occasions if the victim was enjoying the sexual experience. He almost always took trophies of their personal possessions, usually thong panties and bra. Finally, he would ask his victims to shower, so that the evidence of his sexual assault would be washed away.

We, the jurors would most definitely hear all of the problems of Vincent Sanchez' life. The Defense has hinted of them already: A compulsive disorder that leads him to brutalize women in a sexual manner, a drinking problem, a head injury, and a diagnosis of Intermittent Explosive Disorder that allows him to go crazy at a moments notice. However, do these things excuse Vincent Sanchez? Doesn't he have the same power of choice that the rest of mankind has? The choice of good or evil.

SUMMARY OF CRIMES OF THE SIMI VALLEY RAPIST

1. <u>Becky, age 19, crime September 2, 1996</u>. Officer Jones of the Simi Valley Police Department testified on her behalf. Becky was the first known victim of Vincent Sanchez. Her and her mother met the police at a Denny's around 2:22 a.m. to report the crime. Becky told Officer Jones that Sanchez had a knife and threatened to kill her and her grandmother if she did not cooperate (Sanchez thought Becky's mother was her grandmother). Becky had fallen asleep sometime after 10:30 p.m. and was awoken by a knife to her throat. She could not see Sanchez because he had placed a pillow over her face, but she did know he was wearing dark clothing. Sanchez said he knew her from Moorpark College and knew she worked at the Oaks Mall. He forced Becky to have oral sex, raped her twice and sodomized her. He asked her if she was a virgin and what her age was. She stated that he was making threats to her at the beginning of the assaults and again at the end. Once he was gone, they

tried to call police but the phone lines and T.V. power was off.

Sanchez was charged with residential burglary with a knife, two counts of rape with a knife during residential burglary, two counts of forcible oral copulation with a knife during a residential burglary, and one count of forcible sodomy with a knife during a residential burglary. A total of six felony counts.

2. <u>Jinny, age 18, crime June 14, 1997.</u> Jinny was awoken at approximately 4:00 a.m. by Sanchez threatening to kill her with a knife. Sanchez ran out through a window when her father was alerted as Sanchez attempted to take Jinny from the home. Jinny obtained an injury to her knee, but was not molested. An attempt was made to dial 911, but the number was busy. Jinny later realized that he had taken numerous pairs of her thong panties.

Sanchez was charged with attempted kidnap with the intent to rape with a knife.

3. <u>Monica, age 15, crime October 25, 1997.</u> Monica woke up to a noise about 2:36 a.m. and saw Sanchez in a ski mask, gloves and a flashlight in hand. He threatened to kill her parents if she did not stop screaming. She stated she could taste the powder on his latex gloves, as he covered her mouth. Sanchez also placed a pillow over her face. Monica described Sanchez as agitated, as he attempted to take her out of her house. He had shown the flashlight into her mothers' eyes as they went through the hallway. Monica struggled with him and managed to get Sanchez out the door of her house and then shut and locked the door behind him. Her father attempted to chase after him. Luckily, Monica only received a sore neck and throat from screaming. She described her attacker as about 5'8" tall, with thick

dark eyebrows and big arms. She reported that she had heard noise outside her window a few weeks earlier. Later, videotapes revealed that Sanchez had stalked her and taken photos of her changing clothes while in her bedroom. Monica did not report any panties missing.

Sanchez was charged with attempted kidnap with the intent to rape.

4. <u>Lorraine, age 15, crime March 22, 1998.</u> Simi Valley Detective Carrott testified on her behalf. Lorraine was awakened with a pillow placed on her face and a knife at her throat. Lorraine had been sleeping in her panties, which Sanchez asked her to remove. Lorraine then asked Sanchez to put the knife down, which he did. He orally copulated her, but he was unable to keep his erection. Then he began sucking her breasts and asked if she was enjoying it. She stated, "no," to which he replied, "I know you are." Lorraine was shaking severely, when Sanchez said, "calm down. I won't hurt you." He ordered her to perform oral sex on him and raped her. He asked if she was a virgin and when had she last had sex. Lorraine tried to hold his hands so he would not reach for the knife again. Sanchez was wearing a dark ski mask, dark clothing and textured gloves. He then took off the right glove, and turned on her bedroom light. She thought that it was odd that he knew where the switch was because it was in an out of the way place. Sanchez then told her not to look at him and asked her to put on the clothing he had selected. Her mother, father and two sisters were home, sleeping in their own bedrooms. Sanchez warned, "Do you want me to kill your sister?" Lorraine broke free of him and ran toward her parents' bedroom. Sanchez ran out the front door, and Lorraine chased him, but lost him around the corner. She had a cut to her lower lip because of the

pressure he had put on her mouth (she wore braces), and an injury from falling against some furniture. Sanchez had called her "Cat," which was her nickname. While in conversation, he had told Lorraine he did not believe in God because his wife had been taken from him. Thus far, there is no evidence to support this story.

Sanchez was charged with residential burglary with a knife, two counts forcible oral copulation with a knife during the residential burglary, and one count of rape with a knife during the residential burglary. A total of four felony counts.

5. <u>Joyce, age unknown, crime May 4, 1999.</u> Joyce was talking to her boyfriend by phone, when Sanchez charged in her room with a flashlight, shining it in her face and stated, "Shut up, this is the police." Then Sanchez ordered her to turn face down and undress to her panties. He located her car keys and ordered her to go with him. He covered her head with a blanket. Sanchez said, "It is up to you if you live or die." He drove her to a park area near some bushes that already had carpet and a blanket spread down. Sanchez proceeded to photograph her. He then demanded she give him oral sex, licked her breasts, and raped her. He asked Joyce, "How do you like to be fucked?" She stated that he became aggressive and frustrated because he was having trouble keeping an erection. When he moved the crotch of her panties to the side to orally copulate her, she told him she had AIDS, to which he replied, "I have AIDS too." Then he asked her, "Why should I let you live?" She replied, "Because I will not tell." Then Sanchez began talking to her about religion. He asked her if she believed in God? Adolph Hitler? Then he stated very angrily that, "the Jews deserved to die." He told her, "You think you are too good." Joyce wondered

if he knew her from somewhere and was angry with her. Then he asked her for money, took her near her home and told her to wait about five minutes before leaving the car.

When Joyce got to her house, her boyfriend was there with the police. Joyce's injuries were thigh bruises, a cut above her eye, and vaginal area trauma. Sanchez had used a dart gun to subdue her. She was the only Asian victim to date. Later, evidence revealed that he had taken videos outside her window at least a year earlier.

Sanchez was charged with residential burglary with a deadly or dangerous weapon (a dart gun), kidnapping with the intent to rape with a deadly/dangerous weapon (a dart gun), carjacking with the use of a deadly/dangerous weapon, two counts of forcible oral copulation during the commission of a kidnap with a deadly/dangerous weapon, three counts of rape during the commission of a kidnap with a deadly/dangerous weapon, and one count of digital penetration during the commission of a kidnap with a deadly/ dangerous weapon. A total of nine felony counts.

6. <u>Tonya, age 20, crime October 31, 1999.</u> Tonya was grabbed as she got out of her car in the driveway of her home around 1:00 a.m. Her head was covered with a jacket, then she was car-jacked and driven to Sanchez' house. He forced her to undress and to perform oral sex on him, ejaculating in her mouth. He gave her underwear to put on, blindfolded her and took photos. Tonya pleaded with him to not rape her, as she was a virgin. Sanchez became angry when she resisted. He videotaped the rape, which lasted approximately forty-five minutes. He made her take a shower to wash away

any evidence. He asked for money for a cab when he was ready to leave and threatened that she had better not call the police. Her car was returned to her house and he had her count and wait for him to leave the area. Sanchez attempted to act as if they were dating. He asked about her family and her job, and asked if he could spend the night with her. Tonya reported that she had a bra missing, which was later found in his possession.

Sanchez was charged with kidnap with the intent to rape, carjacking, six counts of forcible oral copulation during the commission of a kidnap, one count of forcible oral copulation during the commission of a kidnap with a knife, one count of rape during commission of a kidnap with infliction of great bodily injury, two counts of rape during commission of a kidnap with infliction of great bodily injury with use of a knife, one count forcible digital penetration during the commission of a kidnap, and one count robbery. A total of fourteen felony counts.

7. Connie, age 34, crime February 10, 2000. Connie arrived home around 9:10 p.m. and was surprised that her dog did not greet her. She heard a cell phone ringing, followed the sound into her kitchen, where a man in a ski mask jumped out of a closet and pushed her onto the floor. He straddled her, put a knife to her throat and she began fighting him. He asked, "Do you want to die? Stop fighting!" She stated that it felt as if they struggled for about thirty minutes, at which time he accidentally stabbed her in the calf with the knife, pinning her leg to the floor. Connie gave up the fight when she became exhausted. Sanchez then took his rape bag out of the closet and began using duct tape to bind her wrists. He asked her for money and jewelry and she told him where the safe was. He rummaged through her safe and

purse, found her driver's license and inquired as to her name. He took her class ring, some cash, and some of her grandmother's jewelry. He then stuffed a handful of panties into her mouth and duct taped her mouth. He placed a hood over her head and tightened it around her neck. Connie stated that it appeared he knew some wrestling moves and had a strong upper body. Connie's dog followed them upstairs and lay by her bed. Sanchez told her he would slit her dogs' throat if she did not cooperate. Then he cut the hood off her head and made her perform oral sex on him. He demanded she undress and get in the shower. When the hot water hit her leg, it began to bleed profusely. Sanchez stated, "That could have been your throat." After the shower, he tied a towel around her bleeding leg and had her put on some chosen panties and bra, and pose for photographs. He told her to, "Make it look good, touch yourself. I have nothing to lose, you have everything." Sanchez raped her numerous times and had her perform oral sex on him, as he was having trouble staying erect. He took all of his clothes off except for his mask and video taped the rapes. As Connie was beginning to feel weak from the loss of blood, she told him she needed to go to the hospital. Sanchez had her take a second shower, which he videotaped. He stated he did not want to go to jail, and then got into the shower with her. He looked around her house and found some bandages and applied ice to help slow the bleeding. Following the assaults, he wrapped her in a blanket, offered her a glass of water and gave her the phone to call the police. She froze and said, "no." Then he climbed into bed with her and began rubbing her back. Sanchez talked to her about the Bible. He told her she should read the book of Revelations. "It is a roadmap, the Alpha and Omega, the beginning and the end." Then he told her some far-fetched story about how he had not seen his mother since age seven, had no girlfriend, and had to eat out of trashcans. Sanchez asked for her forgiveness and said that this would never happen again. Connie continued to tell him that she needed to go to the hospital, as she was becoming more dizzy and faint. He gathered up his black rape bag and threatened her not to tell. He took her video camera, forty dollars, a satin change purse and some jewelry. When Connie called 911 for medical care, she did not report that she had been raped, only stabbed and robbed. She later testified that her parents' name and address was on the tag of the stolen video camera bag, and she was afraid he would harm them. The hospital authorities alerted the police, who came to take a report. Connie did not have a sexual assault exam, only treatment for the stab wound on her leg. Other injuries were a knife poke to her buttocks, strained neck, scratches to her hands, back, neck and numerous bruises. One month later, she saw the symbol for the Alpha/Omega written in the dirt on her car.

Sanchez was charged with residential burglary with a knife, robbery of inhabited dwelling with infliction of great bodily injury with a knife, two counts forcible oral copulation during the commission of a residential burglary with a knife, and one count of rape during the commission of a residential burglary with a knife. A total of five felony counts.

8. <u>Judy, age 22, crime March 15, 2000.</u> Judy arrived home about 9:45 p.m. When Sanchez attacked her, she tried to grab the phone but it was knocked away. He was wearing a ski mask, leather jacket and gloves. He threatened to kill her father if she screamed. When she stopped fighting, he calmed down. He had a knife, wrapped in a towel. Judy elbowed him and grabbed the

knife and began swinging it. Sanchez hit her with his fist on the face. As he ran toward the master bedroom, Judy gave chase and pulled his ski mask off. When Sanchez knocked the screen door onto the patio as he exited, Judy saw his profile. She describes him as late 20's, dark brown spiky hair with bleached tips. Judy then ran into her fathers' room and showed the ski mask and knife to him, while her sister called the police. Judy received a cut to her mouth from the struggle. She later discovered that the knife had been taken from her kitchen. Also, she reported that she had a missing black lace bra. Later she identified the bra from a series of bras that had been recovered. Sanchez did not have the duffle bag (sex kit) this time and no videos were taken. Judy's sister told police that she had noticed something suspicious about their storage shed earlier and her father stated that the cats had been acting weird.

Sanchez was charged with residential burglary with a knife and assault with the intent of rape with a knife. A total of two felony counts.

9. <u>Ursula, age 20, crime March 16, 2000</u>. Sanchez struck again the next night at 3:00 a.m. He came into Ursula's bedroom and stated, "It's okay, I'm a police officer." Once she was aware of what was happening, he threatened that he and his buddies would kill her and her family. Ursula stated that he seemed angry and nervous. She asked him if he was going to kill her, to which he replied, "Do you think I am?" Sanchez took thong panties from her drawer and told her to put them on. Ursula stated that she felt camera flashes even though her face was covered. He set up a video camera and had her perform oral sex on him. She stated he had trouble keeping an erection. She asked him to use a condom before he raped her. Sanchez took her out of her house

23

in only panties and a bra and lead her to the backyard. He told her other guys were there and to stay still. Then he took her sweatshirt, shorts, and a cell phone. He then asked Ursula for money.

After parking around the corner and acting as if he was waiting for his friends, Sanchez took her car and they drove with her head covered for about ten to fifteen minutes. He asked her questions about her school, hobbies, and boyfriend. She tried not to upset him after he made a comment about her being "a snobby, pretty girl." Sanchez took her to his house and when Ursula began to cry he got upset. He took two pairs of thong panties out of a duffle bag and told her to put on the white satin ones. He photographed her and then told her to take off her bra. Sanchez attempted to rape her but was having trouble staying erect. He made her give him oral sex and she bite him. Ursula described his demeanor as "bothered, displeased." Sanchez inquired if she was enjoying this experience. Once he had ejaculated, he told her to take a shower, but she refused. He allowed her to use a washcloth to wash herself. Ursula told him she was on her period and he located a Maxi pad for her. He tried to make small talk with her, telling her she should try for a modeling career. He asked her had she ever been pregnant to which she replied, "No, I had an abortion." Ursula arrived back home around 5:30 a.m. and was told to count to twenty before getting out of the car. Her father gets up around 5:00 a.m. and Sanchez agreed he would get her back before her father noticed her missing. Ursula's mother had already began looking for her. Ursula stated she felt that he had been stalking her because he knew her boyfriend drove a truck. Sanchez stated to her, "Girls lie. I would marry you and get you pregnant with lots of kids." He asked her if she was Jehovah's Witness or

Mormon, as he had seen some religious materials in her home. Ursula later discovered the knife he used was taken from her kitchen. She had an assault exam and swabs were taken. Her injuries were soreness, cuts, and bruises.

Sanchez was charged with residential burglary with a knife, two counts of forcible oral copulation during the commission of residential burglary with a knife, one count rape during the commission of residential burglary with a knife, kidnap with intent to rape with a knife, carjacking with a knife, two counts of rape during the commission of kidnap, one count forcible oral copulation during the commission of kidnap. A total of nine felony counts.

10. <u>Annette, age 29, crime November 9, 2000.</u> Annette spoke about having a spooky feeling several times during mid-afternoon. She found her grandfathers' gun on the floor and put it back in the box and then away. She stated she felt someone was there to rob her. Sanchez attacked her with closed fists, and tied her ankles with plastic restraint ties. Once he realized that he had gotten them too tight, he cut them off. He blindfolded her and dragged her to her bedroom. He asked her about school, her father, her name and asked for money. She stated she had fifty dollars on her dresser. Annette had photos in her room of provocative poses of her during her modeling phase and these seemed to excite Sanchez. He threatened to use them to exploit her if he was found out. Annette said she was resistive with him and would curl into a fetal position. He became angry when she was not compliant with him, binding her wrists and called her a "fucking bitch." When he locked her bedroom door and she felt, "this is the time to fight." Annette bit his finger, and hit him with a picture frame.

He slammed her, and hit her in the head with a beer bottle four times. She stated she felt as if he was trying to kill her when he began choking her. Her body went limp but she was not sure if she went unconscious. Annette managed to get free of him again and pushed a table between them, grabbing a metal lamp. Sanchez refused to leave until he found his mask. She felt certain that he had taken photographs of her because she heard the camera. When he was gone, she dialed 911 but the phone was not working. Annette only had a cursory exam at the hospital, which upset her. The police were on hand to interview her. She informed police that she had fifty dollars missing, along with a Minolta camera. She felt she could recognize the perpetrator by his hair, and described an affected Spanish accent. She was not aware of any weapon, which is what allowed her to fight back. Her reported injuries were a loose tooth, cuts and bruises to her face, a back injury, some language and memory loss, and trouble with her eyes.

Sanchez was charged with residential burglary, first degree robbery of an inhabited dwelling, assault with deadly weapon by force likely to produce great bodily injury and infliction of great bodily injury, assault with the intent to rape with use of dangerous and deadly weapon with infliction of great bodily injury, and false imprisonment with violence or menace. A total of five felony counts.

11. <u>Megan Barroso, age 20, crime July 4, 2001.</u> Megan was murdered and her body was dumped in a canyon. There was also possible kidnap and rape involved.

    Sanchez admitted to murdering Megan. Currently, he was being tried for possible kidnapping with intent to rape and facing the death penalty.

12. <u>Donna, age 22, crime July 10, 2001.</u> Donna was walking to her boyfriends' house about one and a half miles away, when Sanchez came out of the bushes and placed a knife at her throat. He said, "Don't scream. Do you have any money?" Then he told her to drop her cell phone into the bushes. She described him as wearing dark clothing and gloves. He drove a Ford Ranger with beige interior. He bound her feet with duct tape and her hands were bound with metal handcuffs. He placed her into the truck through the drivers' side and requested that she give him oral sex. She described his demeanor as "mean, harsh, rough and stern." When she stopped orally copulating him, he responded angrily, "Why are you stopping?" Sanchez took Donna into his garage and cut the tape off her ankles. He led her into his bedroom, where the windows were covered in dark material. He had her remove her clothing and then performed oral sex on her. She begged him to use a condom. She stated she saw his face and eyes when he raped her. He told her, "Your boyfriend is lucky, you're beautiful. I wish we could have met under different circumstances." After the rape, he offered her a Dr. Pepper, and tried to embrace and comfort her. She was trembling and shaken. He assured her he would get her back in time for work in the morning. He covered her face with his sweatshirt and they drove around for about thirty to forty minutes. When they arrived back at the spot where he picked her up, he took a flashlight and looked for her cell phone in the bushes. He had the usual conversation about school, and he asked her about Cal State College. She wondered if they went to the same school. Donna gave her boyfriends' address as her own, and Sanchez became angry when he realized that her driver's license address did not match the one she gave him. Donna told him a story about not having it changed

27

with DMV. Sanchez drove up and down her boyfriends' street, acting as if he was unsure of letting her out. He stated, "I have a funny feeling about this." Donna told him she had been raped before and did not tell, to which he replied, "You're pure." Sanchez stopped short of the house and asked her for a good-bye kiss. He told her she could keep his sweatshirt. Donna's boyfriend called the police when she got inside his home. She was examined at the hospital and later was able to identify Sanchez in a line-up (he had not worn a ski mask this time.) She was also able to give an accurate description of his garage and bedroom. This appeared to be a crime of opportunity, not a stalking incident. This crime happened just five days after Sanchez had killed Megan Barroso. We, the jurors would later discuss that Donna was really lucky to be alive because Sanchez showed some reservation about letting her out of the car.

Sanchez was charged with kidnap with the intent to rape with a knife, three counts of forcible oral copulation during the commission of kidnapping with a knife, one count of rape during the commission of a kidnap with a knife, and robbery with a knife. A total of six felony counts.

SURVIVAL INSTINCT

The jury is made up of twelve citizens, plus an extra five alternates. The reason being that this case is expected to go on for three to four months, and some jurors may be dismissed or have to quit before the end. Being number five alternate means that I have to listen to all the evidence from beginning to end, and may or may not have a vote of the verdict or sentencing. This will prove to be a course in self-discipline for me.

The first few weeks yielded a willingness to work together and be of good cheer. We decided that we would ask about wearing Hawaiian print clothing on Fridays. We had several members who donated cookies, chips, pretzels, and a cake to the cause. We are sure that we will not go hungry. It must be a survival instinct. We learned that we will not be sequestered during the trial but nonetheless, we feel trapped.

Various members brought to the table; mood rings, Internet jokes, and a multitude of stories from all walks of life. Talking about our pets is a safe place to connect. The postal worker told us his experience with many other people's pets. His recall is not as pleasant as those of us who are pet owners.

One of our biggest feats thus far, is to get ourselves lined up in order of our seating arrangement before we enter the courtroom. A female naval intelligence personnel is determined to have us get it right, but she is showing signs of frustration with us already. It seems that we have some very independent individuals working on this jury.

Some of the men have started to assert themselves and want us to make demands to the judge. I feel that Judge Riley made the mistake of telling us how important we were and how much the court would attempt to accommodate us. Bailiff Abbott has also reinforced the idea by stating that we should let them know if we are unhappy about anything in the courtroom. "After all, you people are the most important. You need to be comfortable and clear." I bet he will live to regret that remark.

MID-WEEK

This chapter should be titled, "Things I learned this week." Two really important concepts are to be more alert to things happening around you for your personal safety and the other is to be more aware in general. We have heard twenty-seven witnesses and it is only Wednesday. I am surprised that most of the sexual assault victims have testified. By what we are hearing, it is obvious that many people don't pay attention to details, or process the information that goes past their senses. Many questions were not asked during the investigation that seemed logical to ask. Details about the crimes that were not picked up by officers, investigators, other witnesses and so on. Also, memories that are lost over time. It is nobody's fault, just human nature.

We heard from various experts in their field. We learned how K-9's are trained to track a scent. First they learn on soft surfaces, like dirt. Tracks are made and hotdogs are placed on the tracks. This gives the dog an incentive to participate. After they get this part down, then they learn to do the same on hard surfaces, such as pavement. Did you know that we constantly drop cells from our bodies? Dogs can identify us by this and track our movements. The dog handler puts the dog on a long lead, about 30 feet and "casts" the dog. Casting is to move the lead from side to side to guide the dog while covering a large radius, such as a crime scene. Things that can throw the dog off are: lifting his head, or being distracted, being fatigued, having multiple footprint that contaminate the area, or weather changes, such as wind dispersing scents. In this case, Senior Deputy Hardy of the Ventura County Sheriff's Department was the handler for five-and-a-half-year-old Duro. They searched a fifty-foot radius around the victim's car. Duro went straight to Megan's car door and put his paws on it and then he went straight to her sandal, which was about three feet from the car on the pavement. The K-9 found her scent but was unable to track it past the sandal. There was some speculation that Duro may have been fatigued, since he had worked up until midnight the previous evening. The tracking deputy had arrived at the crime scene with Duro around 4:30 a.m. We, the jurors requested to see a demonstration of the dog's tracking abilities but the judge said he could not order it. If the attorneys felt it relevant, then they could request it. The Prosecutors chuckled at our request and agreed it would be interesting to see this procedure. But alas, no fieldtrip to the K-9 school.

Later, Senior Deputy Godfrey, an accident reconstruction expert, walked through the crime scene measuring the bullet holes, the fields of glass on the roadway, bullet cartridges, bullet fragments, the cleaning rod from an AK-47, and where Megan's sandal laid. He explained how the newer model vehicles have a black box, a brain of sorts that records data as it occurs on the car. This device was developed in the event that the air bag needs to be dispatched. If you hit something or have a sudden hard impact while driving, this brain will decide if it should release the air bag. If it determines that the impact does not require an air bag, it will carry on but continue to provide a permanent record of the event. This data can then be interpreted and is placed on a graph. The black box records all the ignition cycles on the car. Because the data cannot be erased, Deputy Godfrey was able to determine that Megan's Sun Fire was gunned to full throttle from a stopped position. It hit the curb while attempting to turn onto Los Angeles Avenue but soon coasted to a stop on the median, after a sharp left turn. His final explanation was how they re-enact the accident using the information they gather. It was very technical but interesting.

Lastly, an investigator told us how they collect DNA to prove the suspect is guilty or to rule out guilt. At the point when Investigator Schatz told Sanchez that his DNA would be tested, he admitted to the sex crimes against these women. All of the personnel were extremely excited to have found the guy who was now labeled the Simi Valley Rapist. They already had Sanchez in custody for a burglary but it was a few days later before they were alerted to his connection to the sexual crimes. This happened when two of his roommates found a bag of videos, 8mm films, panties, photos, miscellaneous papers, and a photo of his girlfriend hidden in a recycle bin. After viewing some of the videos, the roommates called the police. I wonder how it feels to learn that you shared a house with a person who is capable of these crimes? But worse yet, what about sharing a bed with someone who did this? Sanchez told Investigator Schatz that he did these sexual assaults only when he and his girlfriend, Luz broke up or were fighting.

JUNK, JUNK, AND MORE JUNK

The Prosecution's witnesses have been very credible thus far. We have now heard thirty witnesses and it is the end of the second week of testimony. The bailiff stated that this case seems to be going quickly. I hope he is right.

The last day and a half of this week consisted of a ballistics expert going over the details of the bullet fragments, trajectory, speed of bullets, weight and so on. This appears to be much more detail than we need. After all, we know that Megan was shot by Sanchez, with the A-K 47, using the bullets that were identified at the crime scene. And the holes in the car verify six shots were fired. Ear witnesses also verify that six shots were heard. Do we really need to know how fast the bullet went into Megan, and possibly caused her death? The Chief Defense Attorney, Quinn belabors every point and repeats the same information over and over. AT this point I am still trying to determine what he is accomplishing with this line of questioning, other than to wear out the jurors.

I am very impressed with Mr. Roberts, Ventura County's expert ballistics re-constructionist. He is very detailed, precise and does not let Quinn take him anywhere he does not want to go. He corrects Quinn, when he attempts to put words in his mouth. The Prosecution is becoming irritated with this questioning also, and keeps repeating "objection, that is not the testimony that was given by Mr. Roberts." After talking for a day and a-half, Mr. Roberts was excused for an extended trip that was pre-planned. He will be back in a few weeks to continue his testimony. Judge Riley encouraged the jurors when he stated that we may be in the Defense portion by then. Mr. Roberts will pick up where he left off in his testimony.

I found myself wondering how the court personnel; Judge, Prosecutors, Defense Attorneys, Court reporters, Clerks and Bailiffs can listen to all the gory details in case after case and not go nuts. They must have some real good coping skills in place. I still say a little prayer for them each day as we are going through the proceedings. The witnesses and the victims especially need our prayers. Juror #1 and I have been cleansing the courtroom and the juror's room for negative karma. I have started to question which jurors will not make it to the end of this trial. There are a couple that appear to be having a difficult time. I believe it is because of their personal lives. The thing is, in the jury room we have nothing but ourselves to talk about. We are learning about each other and hoping that when the time comes to really work together, everyone will. Everyone is definitely working to make sure we don't run out of junk food!

SANCHEZ, THE MAN

Vincent Sanchez is this pathetic little man, who has victimized many women. We will probably never know just how many. The Defense is attempting to paint a picture of a guy who will nurture his victims by giving them water or a soda, after he has assaulted them. He was so concerned about them that he asks if they are enjoying the sex acts being forced on them. What a guy! Also, he has apparently coerced his girlfriend, Luz to dress up, or pose nude and let him take photos of her. We have not seen these photos but the act has been insinuated to us. We did view the photos of some of his victims, in the nude or partially dressed. I have a feeling of disdain for him after seeing these photos. The humiliation of these acts must have been horrible. Then to have so many people view them over and over; during investigations, hearings, and the trial. I can understand why rape victims feel they keep getting victimized. Some never tell. If one had an idea of the amount of grief one would encounter, many of us probably would not tell either. I find myself hoping that Sanchez is humiliated when they testify about his actions. He is a small man, with protruding front teeth, who takes what he wants at knife or gunpoint. One cannot help but have animosity towards him. Through some of the testimony, it appears that he targets fifteen-year-old ladies. I consider myself a compassionate person by most standards, but it is very hard to have compassion for him right now. He knew he had a "problem." Why did he not seek help? He told Investigator Schatz that he was doing pretty well while he had a girlfriend. I wonder what abuse he heaped on her? I believe we will hear about that also before this complete story has been told.

After hearing from yet another victim, I have another hero. The eighth victim, Judy fought back. She got the knife from Sanchez and chased him with it. She also pulled off his ski mask. He ran for his life. And as he left her house, she yelled, "don't go, asshole!" This comment even made the Defense Attorney Quinn chuckle. I admit, I did too. Really, all of these women are heroes. To go through something like this and live to talk about it. Hopefully, to live to see your perpetrator pay. Will he pay with his life, or will he "get life?"

RAMBLINGS

So far, all of this rambling has been done inside my head. I knew myself well enough to know that I would go crazy if I could not vent this information for three to four months. So I decided that I would journal my thoughts while sitting alone in the evenings after each day in court. The need to express seems to be a female thing. Most of the women on the jury have started to verbalize some irritation. We got a new bailiff today. Bailiff Abbott has a long over-due vacation to Cabo. The new guy is already getting jabs from some of the women. I guess it is true that women are catty! He seems to be pleasant and friendly, so I am not sure what the others don't like about him. Probably because he is not Abbott. Humans sure get conditioned quickly. The new guy is expected to do things just the way we are used to--like Abbott does them. We are already showing signs of being spoiled!

In discussing how people simulate stressful information, it appears that they just find a target. We cannot really direct our anger at Sanchez because we are supposed to be objective. So we have picked somebody "safe" to resent. I wonder if anyone has done studies on jurors to determine how they cope psychologically to heinous crime evidence. One wonders how we will view life after this case? Will this forever change us? It struck me as strange and sad today, when Connie is pouring out her heart to us about the ordeal she went through with Sanchez. I felt as if we were watching some crazy movie. Boy, are we conditioned to violence or what? I tried to concentrate on the words and really feel her pain. But it seems that my mind would shut down my emotions and take me into some surreal place. Often I would bring my mind back to the pain and ask myself, how does a person endure things like this? How could a person do things like this to anyone? How does Vincent Sanchez' mind work? This is the mystery of this case.

Art Barroso, Megan's father has not shown up in the courtroom since the first few days of the trial. But he showed up in my dream last night. In this dream I was relating to him how sorry I was about Megan, and hoped he was doing okay. Today, late in the afternoon, Art was sitting in the courtroom listening to the last witness of the day. I looked several times in disbelief, as I had not seen him come into the room. This felt really strange to me. Were we communicating telepathetically?

PATTERNS

The Defense stated we would be looking for patterns. And so there are-- many patterns. Patterns in the weapons used, words spoken, stalking behaviors, photographing the victims, appearance of targeted victims, sexual acts performed, clothing worn or requested to be worn, type of places where the victims lived, window dressings on their bedroom windows, demeanor of the perpetrator at different intervals, and his behavior after attacking these women. He frequently asked for money, once to take a cab home. That was quite absurd! Sanchez would steal their possessions, jewelry and undergarments. He had a fetish for thong panties. But there were some exceptions to his patterns as well. For instance, becoming very hostile and aggressive if he did not get his way, or running like a scared rabbit when confronted.

Today was a short work day but extremely intense. The first order of business was to have the jury view one of the videos that Sanchez had taped. The purpose was not to prove that he did the crimes, because he has already confessed to that. But to determine the credibility of Connie (victim

#7), or for impeachment reasons as the Judge explained. This tape was very disturbing. It was like a B-rated porn film. However, the most disturbing part was the fact that it did impeach Connie's testimony in several ways. Both, by her not remembering the facts of what happened and that she did a real good job of "faking it" for the camera. Sanchez had told her to make it look good before he started to film. There were parts in the video when it looked as if she were the aggressor in the sex acts. I guess that sounds really judgmental, and I do realize she felt she was giving the performance of her life. Or for her life. Connie stated earlier in her testimony that she just wanted to get it over with. This video did not help the People's case, at any rate.

Two of Megan's friends testified late morning. It was sad to hear them talk about the last evening they had spent with Megan alive. Just a group of young kids going from party to party to make the most of the July fourth holiday. They met and walked along Silver Strand Beach with friends, had some drinks and later, went to another friends house for milk shakes. One of the girls had red fairy dust that she blew on everyone. Their final stop was to pick up their cars at Kimberly's house. They disbursed around 3:00 a.m. in preparation for a trip several of them were taking up north the following day. Megan jumped on her friend, Kimberly and gave her a final hug. When she did this, she knocked her purse into the ground and it's contents fell out. One of the girls picked them up and inadvertently placed Kimberly's cell phone into Megan's purse.

In the afternoon, the courtroom was dark because one of the jurors needed to see a doctor. He had gotten in an auto accident on the way to court the previous morning. After much encouragement from us, and him feeling like a Mac truck had hit him, he decided it might be a good idea to get checked out. Nothing like a good shopping trip to take a gal's mind off gruesome details. It worked for me anyway. The mind really needs time to rest and focus on other things, healthy things. I am attempting to use this time for self-improvement: reading, yoga, exercise, self-help tapes and shopping. I seem to be getting a taste of what it might feel like to be semi-retired. We have had many starts and stops in this case thus far. I can begin to see why the court predicted it might be mid-August before we finish.

TONYA'S TRAUMA

Wednesday morning started out well. Josh Reno, Sanchez' roommate testified. He was an apprehensive young guy who worked as a grip for the studios. He was very blunt and for that reason, a lot of what he said was funny. He even had the Judge laughing out loud. At one point Chief Prosecuting Attorney, Dobroth stated she was almost afraid to ask the next question. Juror #1 had the habit of giving people nicknames. Josh Reno' was Kato, and he really did resemble that character.

But all things come to an end, and so by the afternoon we were viewing Megan's decomposed body. Mr. Clark, a civilian Search and Rescue for Ventura County testified about going into Black Canyon and finding the remains. Actually, Bella, a trained K-9 and her handler, Mrs. Teller, found Megan. They have worked together for some time and were very experienced in finding human remains. Some of their experience was having searched for bodies at the World Trade Center bombing. Bella is trained to find dead or alive human bodies. It was interesting to note that these dogs are trained not to "alert" to animals remains. Alert means when the dog senses they have found something, they will go in circles and then sit. This is so they don't disturb any of the crime scene. Mrs. Teller stated that the reason they had gone into that ravine was because one could smell an odor of decay. I have really enjoyed learning how the experts work.

Once Bella and Mrs. Teller found where the odor was coming from, Mr. Clark uncovered the body and identified that is was in fact, human. Mr. Clark alerted his teammate up on the roadway that they needed to notify the Command Post. He was pretty sure that it was Megan Barroso because he had been told what clothing to look for and details about her ring and bracelet.

To end the day, we had to watch another videotape. This time is was Tonya (victim #6) and the whole scene looked completely different. For one, Sanchez had his face showing throughout the filming. He made her wear a blindfold and put a pillow over her face. It was very clear to us that it was him performing the assaults, as he was not wearing his mask and actually looked into the camera. Tonya was timid, tense and pleaded with him throughout the video to stop. She also told him she was a virgin and was in a lot of pain. It was obvious that she was because her body was contracting the whole time. She pleaded with him not to rape her. He raped her numerous times and made her orally copulate him. Then he ejaculated in her mouth. I felt as if I was being raped! This tape seemed to go on for a very long time. I wanted to just scream, "stop this!" Now, I understand why victims cannot give good time frames. When you are being victimized it seems endless. I believe this film went on for about forty minutes. Sanchez elected not to be in the courtroom while these tapes were being shown. And I thought he was so proud of his production. Why else would he videotape it?

The group was very solemn upon leaving the courtroom. No one talked at all, but made a mad dash from the building. I left with a tension headache and later realized it was because I had been clenching my teeth and tensing my body during the entire viewing of the rape video. I felt dirty, needing to wash off the stench. I soaked in a hot tub and was relieved that there was some mindless entertainment on T.V. that evening. I watched the final episode of American Idol and went to bed early.

My feelings were hard to shake. I was angry, stunned, tense and sad. I later found out that one of the males from the jury was extremely angry and another went to his car and "cried his eyes out." He said all he wanted to do all evening was rant. This is only a small sampling of the pain that Sanchez has caused so many people. I find myself wondering how Tonya deals with this experience in her present life.

KIMBERLY'S TESTIMONY

Today, we heard testimony from one of Megan's best friends, Kimberly. She supplied a lot of details. The type that only a best girlfriend could. She discussed Megan's driving habits, music she liked best and listened to, the clothes Megan owned, her sizes, her weight, what her makeup bag looked like, contents of her purse and her cell phone with sticker attached that read "angry girl." And even the type of feminine hygiene products Megan used.

Kimberly has a history of depression and had been diagnosed Bi-polar at age seventeen. The Prosecution brought this out first because they knew the Defense would. Kimberly got very depressed in November 2001, following the death of Megan, which it seems she felt responsible for. She stated that she felt that if Megan had not come back to bring her cell phone that accidentally got placed in Megan's purse, she would still be alive. Kimberly was hospitalized several times over the next few months. By February 2002, she was doing well and had a "good therapist." She was also receiving grief counseling.

Kimberly is a key witness in this case and for this reason, Defense Attorney Quinn spent the rest of her testimony attempting to impeach her. Quinn was able to point out some discrepancies in the way she stated things in her earlier interviews with officers and the way she states them now. But the content was not significantly different. After all, numerous officers, investigators, Defense personnel, and Prosecuting personnel had interviewed her. Could any of us remember the exact words we used each and every time? I think the Defense was annoyed at just how much she did remember. Kimberly's story was that Megan had joined her at a family B.B.Q. Once there, Megan realized she had started her menses and spotted on her white Capri pants. With Kimberly's assistance, Megan used Spray-n-wash to clean them by hand. Kimberly noted that Megan was wearing white cotton panties. She called them "granny panties." There were some inconsistencies to the order of events but basically I feel these were the most important elements. The issue of what panties Megan was wearing came up later, when she was found in thong underwear and no outer pants. Sanchez was known to have a fetish for thong panties, and usually had his victims wear them. Since the Special Circumstances hangs on the possibility of kidnap to rape of Megan, Kimberly's testimony was very important. So was her credibility.

Kimberly held her own with Quinn, even though she had been testifying for almost two days. He did do what I had suspected that he would, attack her credibility because of her needing and receiving mental health services. That really did not shake her either. He made his biggest mistake when he asked how she felt about Sanchez. Kimberly asked to move the screen that was standing in the view of Sanchez so she could see his face. Then she made eye contact with him and stated, "Hello Vincent, will you look at me." This was the first and only time thus far that he had looked up or made eye contact with anyone! She stumbled over the words but basically stated, "She did not hate him, only some of the things he had done." She went on to say that she felt Megan would not wish any harm to him either. By this point, I cast my eyes downward because I could feel the emotion welling up inside me. It was touching to me because this young girl who had lost her best friend, was able to show kindness to Vincent. This was the same young lady who had been hospitalized after her best friend had been murdered. Kimberly was showing signs of forgiveness. I believe she does have a good therapist!

I was unable to see what Sanchez' reaction was at this time, but there was a hush over the courtroom that was as thick as this morning's fog. Shortly after that, Quinn had no more questions for Kimberly and she stepped down from the stand. The Judge spoke with us about our long weekend and how rough this week had been. He also told us to be safe and expect another rough one in the coming week.

WHAT HAPPENED TO MEGAN'S CAPRIS?

This week started out well, after a long Memorial Day weekend. I had company most of the weekend and really enjoyed hearing someone else talk about their life. Also, I had a chance to relax and soak up some sun and fun. Tuesday was spent with eight or so witnesses that worked on the Search and Rescue operations for Megan's remains. The Search and Rescue coordinator informs us that some 300 people had searched for Megan over the period of one month. It is ironic that she disappeared on July fourth weekend and was found August fifth. The point of all this testimony today was to establish that her white Capri pants were never found. According to two experts, this is highly unusual. If any wild animals were involved in the desecration of her remains, the animal would not carry the clothing off. They would have no interest in the clothing. Their goal would be to remove the flesh. One expert testified that in his thirty years of work, he has never seen a case where the clothing was not located. This led him to believe that the pants were not on the body of Megan when she was dumped there. This is very damaging information for the Defense. They are attempting to paint the picture that Sanchez shot her and just dumped her body. If it is established that he did in fact kidnap and rape her, he is eligible for the death penalty, under Special Circumstances.

The way the story reads so far...Sanchez was very angry on July fourth because his girlfriend, Luz was at her sister's party and so was Luz' ex-husband. Sanchez was not invited and he was very upset about not getting to spend the holiday with her. He had stolen an AK-47 from his roommate, Josh and had it in his truck as he drove the highways around 118 and the 23 freeway. It was presumed that he was on his way to Luz's sisters house. Somehow, he met up with Megan on the roadway. It is believed by the Prosecution that he side-swapped Megan's rental car and waited at the intersection with the gun. When Megan stopped at the 118/23 off-ramp, Sanchez shot into her car approximately six times. At least one bullet hit her and lodged in her back near the spine. They are not clear if Megan got out of the car on her own volition or if Sanchez carried her. One sandal was left in the car and one was found on the pavement near the abandoned car. Megan's purse, cell phone, and makeup bag were also left behind. No one saw Megan after that so it is not clear when she died. The Prosecution believes that Sanchez took her somewhere and had her change into thong panties. That is what she was wearing when the remains of her body were found a month later in Black Canyon. It is believed that she did not have the white Capri pants on that she had been wearing earlier that evening. These pants were never recovered.

We have not heard the Defenses story yet, but it appears that they are attempting to establish that Sanchez had an anger problem and was very upset about breaking up with his girlfriend. They seem to think that he might have had some type of traffic confrontation with Megan while on the roadway. Sanchez was known to be hot-headed and he may have retaliated by using the gun on her. The Defense has already conceded that he did shoot her but implies that it was his explosive reaction that leads him to do so. Of course, they do not want us to believe that he lay-in-wait for her or did anything with her body except to dump it in the ravine. They are trying to save his life, after all.

DEPRESSION AND DESPAIR

I have begun to realize why I was selected for this jury. I have an extensive history in Mental Health, with people who need a lot of care and attention. Vincent Sanchez is definitely that type of person. After hearing his half brother, Anthony testify, it is clear just how needy Vincent was. Anthony testified about the volatile relationship that Vincent had with Luz, how he was depressed, being out of work and having an injury that he expected to receive money for. Anthony spent about three months with Vincent, attempting to get him stable. He took him to Mental Health and had Vincent admitted twice. But Vincent did not want to stay and left before it was advised that he do so. Mental Health discharged him with medication and for a period of time he remained stable. But typical of this type of disability, he stopped his medication at some point. Vincent did as most depressives do; he went in and out of depression and despair. It was hard for those close to him to realize just how much help he really needed. One cannot help but have compassion for a person who is so troubled. Vincent tried to tell his best friend, George. He got drunk one night and all but told George of his plans to kill someone. Vincent confided, "I have done some really bad things. Things I can not tell you about because you would not understand or like me anymore." He went on to say, "I am so angry that I feel like I would like to just open fire on someone, maybe a cop." He even waved the AK-47 (that he stole from Josh) in the air and pretended to aim it at a car coming down his street. Vincent admitted that he had thought about suicide and had put a gun in his mouth on one occasion. He spoke about his frustration with Luz and not having work. Most of the people who knew him just wrote it off that his problems were because he and Luz were having hard times. His brother knew how bad their relationship was because he interceded on several occasions. Luz told him that she was afraid of Vincent and that he might try to kill her. On one occasion, Vincent had a shotgun hid when he went to meet Luz. Anthony made him give up the gun and turned it in to the police. Luz had taken the steps to get a restraining order against Vincent. The question was asked, "Why didn't Vincent accept psychiatric help or counseling?" According to his brother, Vincent was not able to receive any counseling at Mental Health, only medication. If this is true, then we are truly failing as a humane society.

George, Vincent's friend was an adverse witness in this trial. Meaning, he was testifying against his will. He stated that he still considered Vincent a good friend and did not want to be a part of anything that could decide that Vincent would get the death penalty. His testimony however, was damaging to Vincent's case. Vincent told George about the AK-47, wanting to kill someone; even showing George places in the canyon that are "good places to hide a body." It sounded to me that this dialogue indicated that Vincent was putting all the parts together to commit a very serious crime. Most of this conversation was about a week before he actually did commit a serious crime, killing Megan Barroso. It really is sad when one can see in retrospect, that he was slowly unraveling. His roommates had testified that Vincent had gotten to the point of staying in his room. He had a dark curtain over the windows where no light could come in and he didn't even turn on the lights in his room. This was occurring a number of months before Megan's murder. As the story is told, it sounds as though Vincent was feeling guilt and remorseful for his crimes but could not stop himself. He told George that he would not care if the cops opened fire on him and shot him. Vincent is a sad, pathetic man and it is a shame that he was not stopped before he hurt so many people. It seems obvious that he was crying out for help on numerous occasions. But still-- what about his responsibility for his actions? If he knew he was sick and hurting people, why did he not check himself into treatment and stay with it? Why didn't he go the extra mile to let someone know they had to stop him, if he could not do it himself? Why did he stop taking his medications when he knew he needed them and they helped him to cope? Sounds like he was playing a victim's game. He does not show much, if any self-esteem. He has only looked up twice in the courtroom. Once when Kimberly called him by name and addressed him directly, and once when his brother came into the courtroom. He has only smiled twice; once when his roommate, Josh stated, "Vince could spot a girl wearing a thong at fifty yards." And when his friend, George said that a group hug, "wouldn't look right," after he and Vincent's roommate, Steve consoled Vincent one evening. In Vincent's defense, he did try to slow down on his drinking. He knew that he was not supposed to drink and take medication. Also, Luz got mad at him when he drank. Sounds like the burden of their relationship was too much for Luz. She must feel pretty luck to be alive today!

FORENSIC SCIENCE

It was difficult watching Anthony tell the story of how he tried to help his brother. Anthony was stationed in Libya and had probably flown most of the night to testify in court. They kept him for most of two days, asking some of the same questions in various ways. It was evident that he was very weary the second day of his testimony. I imagined that this was difficult for him also because he was a marine, very disciplined and held a position of prestige at the Embassy. He did appear to be a caring brother but after awhile he just got exasperated with Vincent not putting out enough effort. Anthony admitted that he could not see any reason why Vincent had not continued to work. Or why he did not take his medications, or why he would not stay in Mental Health and receive treatment. Or why he insisted on trying to continue to have a relationship with Luz since she appeared to be so bad for him. Anthony witnessed the pain and frustration that Vincent went through while attempting to please Luz and how inadequate Vincent felt when he could not. His brother also felt that Luz took advantage of Vincent by taking his Suburban and giving him her Ford Ranger. At one point, Vincent was so upset with Luz that he tried to pick up a beer keg and throw it at the Suburban.

One of his friends made him see the foolishness of that, since it was his truck he was damaging. Vincent definitely had an unhealthy fixation on Luz.

Anthony also talked about how estranged other family members were with Vincent.

His parents came to visit him one time while he was in Mental Health. Vincent had a sister whom he had a falling-out with. His sister in the Simi Valley area hardly ever saw him. We have yet to hear the story of Vincent's past life but I suspect the Defense plans to tell us about the family dynamics.

One piece of information that was particularly troubling to me was, that Vincent had been within a mile of my home the day before he killed Megan. One does not think of how often one might come in close contact with danger and not even know it.

The remainder of the day and into the next, was spent listening to Ventura County's Chief Coroner, Dr. O'Halloran. He was a forensic pathologist and a physician of twenty-four years, having autopsied approximately 6,000 bodies. His slow, calm voice reminded me of Mr. Rodgers. He sort of looked like him too. I was impressed with his professional demeanor and his complete confidence in his opinions. One would guess that he has dealt with attorneys many times, as he does not let them sway him from his testimony. It was interesting to learn how he does his job. (My description is very clinical and not meant to offend). We heard all about how the body of Megan was examined, and the conclusions that were reached about the cause of death. His theory was that the probable cause of death was a gunshot wound to the abdomen. The most troubling part was that she probably did not die right away. He testified that she might have lived up to hours or maybe even days.

Megan's body may have lay in the ravine while she was still alive. After much discussion about the position her body was found in, it seemed to me that it was in a position of comfort, like she might be going to sleep. The forensic photographs revealed her body was found lying to one side with her left arm across her body and meeting the right arm that was positioned up around her head. The coroner did not feel that she was paralyzed when the bullet lodged near her spine and that she was probably conscious for a time, as the bleeding would be fairly slow and internal. Dr. O'Halloran did not feel that there was any evidence to support the bullet hitting a major blood vessel. He went on to say that he felt if she had gotten medical attention without the half-hour she would have had a good chance of surviving. This is real bad news for Vincent and his Defense team. He had yet another chance to choose to do the right thing. He could have taken her for medical care but did not.

When the Coroner began to tell how the body decomposes, it was hard to place a real person in that body. Within four hours of death the muscles start to become rigid. The process of rigiamortis sets in. The blood will pool to the lowest point. So if a person is laying with their legs down hill, the blood will pool in the lower extremities. The intestines will bloat and swell up before the body fluids dehydrate. Then insects and animals will began to eat at the flesh. Larger animals, such as coyotes will attempt to pull parts of the body away. In this case, the feet were missing and there was evidence that the leg bones had been chewed on. With further decay, the skin starts to become rubbery and mummified. Dr. O'Halloran testified that it would be very unlikely that forensics could retrieve any DNA such as sperm from the body at this time. Even the panties and T-shirt had so much body fluid stains from decomposer that no blood or semen was found. No genital tissue remained and no DNA would remain after bacterial feeding. His x-rays revealed that Megan had three larger metal fragments in her body; two were located about two inches from the spine and one near the left hip. There was no injury to the spine, and no evidence that the fragments hit the aorta or any major organs. The doctor addressed the possibility that a fragment could have hit the left kidney, as many people's left kidney sits lower than the right. The kidney also moves up and down as we breathe. He felt it was unlikely that Megan was dead before she was removed from her car. Also, there were eight tiny metal pieces where the stomach would have been but impossible to tell if from a bullet or metal from the car. In her right hand, there were specks of what could have been metal or even rock. She was wearing a bracelet and ring on the injured hand. Also she had a tongue ring that showed up on the x-ray but the doctor testified that he became frustrated when he was unable to retrieve it. He thought that it might have gone up into the sinus cavity when he probed the skull. What a job! I guess it is a blessing that someone can do it. It is becoming apparent that there are some things about this case that will never be revealed. If only there was a way Megan could help. Would Vincent?

The Defense wanted to pursue the theory that a partial piece of the bullet fragment pushed through the wall of the aorta and was washed down the blood vessel and lost. This theory might account for why the last fragments were not found. The theory is known as a bullet embolism and is extremely rare. Dr. O'Halloran stated that he had only seen two to three of these cases in over five hundred autopsies. Believing this theory might help to exonerate Sanchez, because if she died before leaving the car he would not be guilty of kidnap, or attempt to rape. (The law states you cannot be found guilty of kidnap if the person is already dead). Dr. O'Halloran stated that the longer it takes to find the body, the less accurate the time of death can be fixed. He finished by stating that Megan could have bled a lot but it would have stayed in the internal cavity.

THE SCIENCE OF DNA

The next testimony would be the forensic scientist who collected trace evidence and tested it for possible DNA, and the DNA specialist who tested to verify DNA. They were both very detailed and precise. I guess, being a scientist makes you that way. Both young ladies appeared to have had experience testifying or had been told how to prepare for it. They were ready with their reports and findings and had good recall about their part in this investigation. The possibility of blood DNA was found in the Ford Ranger and truck bed, in the Sun Fire (Megan's rental car), Megan's purse , make-up bag and at Megan's home. Sanchez' hair samples and sperm were also retrieved and tested. Megan's tooth was used for a reference sample of her DNA. Sanchez' DNA was obtained from a cheek swab.

The science of DNA is very interesting but complex. To get the DNA from Megan, the specialist tried three areas; muscle from the decomposing body, hair follicles, and a tooth. There are three reasons why DNA cannot be obtained from a sample: not enough sample to profile, no DNA present in the sample, or something interfering with the sample, such as dirt, dyes, bacteria or chemicals. (Upholstery cleaner would do this). There are many things that can interfere with the obtaining of enough DNA to run a STR, or Short Tandem Repeat. This is the process used at the Ventura County Crime Lab. To describe it as simply as possible, it is done by measuring the lengths of the DNA marks to any given sample. The DNA was extracted from Megan's tooth by freezing the tooth and then grinding it down into a powder. The actual DNA comes from the core of the tooth. In order to get DNA from a hair strand, the expert tries to find one with root follicles attached or some tissue attached. There is a separate DNA process for hair that does not have tissue attached. Ventura County sends this type out of their lab for testing. Without getting too technical, the bottom line is that they found blood evidence of Megan's DNA in the Ford Ranger, which means she was in Sanchez' truck that night after being shot. Blood was found on the gear stick boot, passenger seat, and various places in the truck and in the truck bed. Red pixie glitter was also found in the truck bed of the Ranger. They were unable to get DNA confirmed on all of their suspected samples. The cleaning of the Ford Ranger may have made it hard to get blood samples but with the technology of science, they used processes to verify the probably of blood present. The techniques are called Luminal and Phenpholain testing. Phenpholain is used with a piece of filter paper or by swabbing a suspected area. If blood is present, there will be a bright color change to fuchsia on the sample when three chemicals are added. Luminal is done in a dark setting, and the area is sprayed with a chemical. If blood is present, the sample will turn a deep blue in color. These tests are done to verify that there is a possibility of blood present when it is not seen by the naked eye. Of course, blood seen by the naked eye is swabbed, collected and preserved for DNA testing in the lab. Some of the DNA samples were so tiny that they could only be tested once. If there were a request for a second test, it would be impossible to get a second result. The experts can add volume to a sample making it possible to get more of a sample, but they cannot duplicate it.

Both of these scientists did a good job of explaining the processes to a group of people who know little about anything so technical. I have been impressed thus far with many of the expert witnesses because of their professional know-how and their ability to relate their work to a group of jurors from various backgrounds.

The forensic experts did extensive testing, including Megan's nail clippings, her cell phone, a rear-view mirror from the Ranger that was found laying on the seat, a tampon applicator found in Megan's apartment, blood spots on her bathroom floor, nail scrapings and cheek swab from Ursula (victim #9), the cleaning rod from the AK-47 found in the 118/23 intersection, pieces of glass with blood on them, and bullet cartridges and casings. They also tested a menstrual pad found in Kimberly's house believed to be Megan's. Later, it was determined it belong to Kimberly's sister. Forensics also took swabs of Kimberly and her sister for DNA samples.

Our last witness this week was an accident re-constructionist. Mr. Rusty Haight evaluated physical evidence from the roadway, photographs of the crime scene, the data report from the Black Box, and a diagram of the scene. He drove a similar car as the Sun Fire and re-enacted the data found on the Black Box. Data reflected that a stop was made at the end of the freeway off-ramp, then a sudden exceleration onto Los Angeles Avenue. Megan's car clipped the center divide as she turned and it was recorded as an impact on the recorder. Within minutes, the car began to decelerate and made a sharp left turn, coasting onto the median before resting there. Mr. Haight helped to create a computer-generated video of the likely events that occurred up to and at the scene. The Prosecution's theory was that somewhere along the freeway, the Sun Fire and the Ford Ranger collided, leaving a scrape along the left side of the Sun Fire. Evidence revealed that the Ford Ranger had been damaged on the right side and the bumper guard was missing. Mr. Haight testified that the Sun Fire had to be traveling faster than the Ranger. He has personally crash-tested around one thousand cars and was the driver of 724 of those at the time they were crashed. The highest speed to date that he crash tested while driving, was 52 m.p.h. He has not talked about any broken bones so far. Haight was the first witness to tell Quinn that he was, "asking questions that were not answerable." Quinn continues to ask the same question several times and several different ways, in an attempt to get someone on record to say something different. I guess it is his job but it is very annoying, nonetheless. The Prosecution got so annoyed with him today that it seemed they would go to blows. Jokingly, I asked the bailiff if he has ever had to handcuff any attorneys to which he replied, "once." Abbott's humor is so dry that I am not sure if he was serious or not.

The end of this week was eventful, as the Judge sent us home early because of a shooting in the courthouse parking lot. Apparently some guy was angry, loaded on Meth and fired three rounds into the air. The police caught him a few blocks away and arrested him at gunpoint. He is now being charged with discharging a weapon and driving under the influence. I did not realize how volatile people in and around the courthouse really are. Which leads me to the next question, why would anyone want to do this job?

THE JURY

This chapter is devoted to my impressions of the personnel and jurors in the courtroom.

Judge Ken Riley: I like very much. He is funny, congenial, and thoughtful. He tries to accommodate the jurors in an effort to keep us happy and patient with the process. He also explains things to us so we don't feel we are left in the dark, i.e., why we are not called in until 9:30 when we are expected to be there at 9:00 a.m. He did give us a pep talk in the fifth week. He was concerned that some of the jurors were getting impatient and/or having personal issues. He reminded us of our commitment to the court and encouraged us that the case was moving along well. Knowing that there is some light at the end of the tunnel helps to keep us from starting to turn on each other (I hope). He predicted that the Prosecution might wrap up their portion by the end of the seventh week.

Chief Deputy Public Defender Neil Quinn: He is quite bright, although one would not suspect it at times. He has a bumbling, Colombo style. It is as if he is trying to act like he does not understand, to throw the witnesses off balance.

He reminds me of a chess player, thinking about three moves ahead. He is very detailed and that is a good quality. But his attempt to testify or change testimony is not very becoming. I sometimes wonder why the Prosecution does not object more often. Maybe they think like I do, that he is just shooting himself in the foot. He has been good about focusing on details that need to be brought out or clarified. He has also softened a bit since the start of the trial. I think maybe his partner told him that he was not winning friends or influencing people, in the right way. He has taken to showing his more personable side, by smiling, joking and sharing his quick wit. This is a much-improved approach to getting others to listen to him.

Deputy Public Defender Jan Helfrich: She is bright, clear, and likeable. She exhibits a good rapport with her client, Sanchez. When she asks questions, she makes it clear what she wants and usually gets it. She has a very direct style and shows her personality as well. Her smile is easy and she gives good eye contact when speaking. She is professional and probably is the most poker-faced of all the attorneys. It is often hard to read how she perceives any given situation. The only way I can tell she is upset is her neck starts to turn red.

Prosecuting Attorney Dee Corona: She is very straightforward and confident. Her quiet, calm style is very deliberate. She does not attempt to hide her disapproval with the Defense tactics. She uses a laid back, matter-o-fact style to voice her objections. Her patience/tolerance level is much higher than mine! But she has probably done this job for many years now. She is very clear when it comes to driving her point home. The witnesses seem to deliver just the way she expects them to. She always reinforces their efforts with a smile and a thank you. She reminds me of a good tennis player in the manner in which she just lobes in her comments.

Chief Prosecutor Lela Henke-Dobroth: She is curt and spunky. One can almost see the fire in her eyes when she feels the Defense is stepping on toes. She is a bit hotheaded but it makes for some very entertaining moments and gives the jurors a wakeup call. She does not leave any rock unturned or any question unanswered. I feel like all my questions are answered by the time she finishes with a witness, except the ones that cannot be answered. She is a professional and a smart-dresser. I like the passion she shows for her job.

Overall, I have been very impressed with the team of professionals in the courtroom.

Even our bailiff, Abbott. He is very friendly and relaxed but will take charge when needed. Because he is young, I think we tend to not take him seriously but he has demonstrated that he is quite competent. As a matter of fact, we like him so much that we have not been very nice to some of the other bailiffs who have filled in during his absence. I believe Abbott is the right person to deal with this group of jurors.

The jurors: We are a group of strong and opinionated people. Most members are bright and quick-witted. We have been having fun joking and getting laughs at each other's expense. Most all, are good-natured about it and it sure helps to cut the tension and stress we are under. As a group, we seem to be holding up to the detailed and upsetting information that we have been exposed to thus far. Individually, not as well….

Juror #1: She is very bright, a teacher of junior high students. Her smile and laughter come easy and she blends well with the group. She has a very spiritual side that she shares with me by trading books and self-help information. Both her and I have "blessed" the group, the courtroom, personnel and the witnesses because there is so much negativity in the area. She works hard to care for her own emotions by taking time for herself after leaving the courthouse. She is a no-nonsense type of person and task-orientated.

Juror #2: A bit older and more experienced than some of us. She has a calming effect on the group. Her past experience serving on a jury will probably make her a very valuable member when it comes to deliberations. If I have the opportunity to vote for foremen, I feel she should be the one. She also has a mothering side, as demonstrated by her shopping for the group. She has a kind heart and nurtures others.

Juror #3: She is an older woman who has had many years of experience in the military and as a sales representative. She is much traveled, and congenial. Some of the jurors have made her a target for jabs as she is most always late to the courtroom, dropping her things on the floor five or six times a day, and walking straight into the line of fire by one or several jurors. She takes it all in stride, is good-natured and has shown more effort to get to court on time.

Juror #4: We call him Biker Bob. Of course that is not his real name. He is out-spoken and assertive, and has become our spokesperson for potty breaks. We joke that the court probably thinks he has the world's smallest bladder. It works for us, because he is centrally located and at eye level with Judge Riley. He has a strong personality, and heaven help us if we disagree with his views come deliberation time. He will maintain his position until the end of time, I believe. He has a mature attitude and seems to have more patience with the process than most.

Juror #5: I call her Amber Alert. Several of us have been alerted to her personality. She is young and a bit immature in her reactions to things. When one juror was obviously upset after testimony one day, her concerned was that she was being ignored. When told that he was just upset and not wanting to talk right then, she stated, "Well, he told the court he could handle this stuff." The truth is, everybody has his or her own way of handling emotional information. She is very bright but sometimes takes herself too seriously. She also exhibits a bit of arrogance and occasionally makes condescending remarks to one of the younger girls.

Juror #6: The surfing association is well represented here. He is pleasant and does not seem to impose himself on anyone. He smiles a lot and mainly talks about his experiences surfing with other surfers in the group. I have not gotten to know him very well but do know that he has a good sense of humor and catches many subtleties in the room.

Juror # 7: "Bad" Paul we call him. I think he actually gave himself that title the first day. He is really the nicest man, an older gentleman. He smiles and jokes a lot and drinks coffee all day. He stands back in the jurors' room and takes everything in.

Juror # 8: He is the one I vote most likely to leave the jury before the end. He has made remarks that indicate that he does not want to be here. I believe people in general do that about jury service so I think that it is expected. But he has already had several issues come up, and I think the Judge has talked to him about whether he can hang with it. He was in an auto accident about the second week of service but luckily he was not hurt too badly to continue. About a year ago he had a surgical procedure to correct his weight problem and has lost 248 lbs. This weighs heavy on his psyche and many issues go unresolved with those close to him. I know this because he is quite candid about it. I enjoy talking to him and experiencing his wit.

Juror #9: The first day he was the one to say, "Does anyone make homemade cookies?" So I blame it on him that I have gained about five pounds since the start of this case. He was very quiet at first, but recently is moving around in the jury room and interacting with more of the jurors. He is an interesting man and I value his perspective.

Juror #10: "Bad, bad Bob" I call him. He is retired and is always asking can we get the day off (only joking of course). He, juror #1 and I eat lunch together many days and then walk the perimeters of the courtyard. He is quick to laugh and get crazy jabs. Therefore, I think he is great. However, he can be serious when the time comes to do so and he will be someone to reckon with at deliberation time. His life has been spent traveling the world and working with quality control. I believe he will help to keep some quality in this group.

Juror #11: Everyone has pet names it seems. His is, "Dan the Man." I gave him that name when I heard about his obsession with the surf. He will go out and check the surf during breaks from the courtroom. He approaches his duty in the courtroom with the same determination. I believe he is the only one who takes as many notes as I do. He also shared that he is an ex-Vietnam vet. He was very solemn during the AK-47 testimony.

Juror # 12: This lady is a real lady. She works in mental health, so her and I have an understanding. We just look at each other at times and seem to know what the other is thinking. She is pleasant and seems to enjoy the group as a whole. However, she like myself has been concerned about some of the pettiness that we have heard recently. She encouraged me to mention it to the bailiff, in hopes that it would be squashed promptly. She understands a lot about human nature but does not like to see people be troublesome.

Alternate Juror #1: He is a young man that works for the postal service. So you can bet that there are many cracks about "going postal." He is fun-loving and colorful. He always has a story to share or a wisecrack to throw out. I enjoy talking with him because he has the ability to help keep things light. Our wisecracks toward him are taken in good humor. He refers to himself as the token hispanic of the group.

Alternate Juror #2: She is a young lady who is sharp and seems to be worldly. She is very capable but does not seem to be assured of herself. For this reason, Juror #5 seems to enjoy giving her a dig now and again. I am not sure if there is a competition of sorts between them. At the beginning, they spent time together and were friendly. Now they hardly talk at all. I enjoy this alternate because we share stories about our dogs. She is very sentimentally attached to her animals, as I am. Recently, she was upset that her dogs had gotten out of the yard before she had to leave for court. This only set the pace for her day and made it more difficult to deal with the irritations of her old friend, Juror #5. This is why I spoke to the bailiff. I felt their riff could make a problem later for the rest of us.

Alternate # 3: He calls himself, "good Paul." I sure don't know why. I have recently tried to help him to see the light about himself, but to no avail. He is fun loving and talkative. The bailiff enjoys him too, I believe. He was right when he stated that he is a true cookie monster. But it is only fair to say that he did make that clear from the beginning. I like him a lot and enjoy his humor and smiling face each day.

Alternate #4: This guy works for the CIA, I believe. He is very quiet and secretive.

Mostly it is because he likes to play with his palm pilot. I tease him about what he is writing about me, but he just smiles and does not divulge anything. Then he will quickly enter something like solitaire on the screen before he shows me that, in fact he is not writing about me. But seriously, we really don't know what he is thinking about this group because he is quiet and shows very little affect. He works with computers in his profession.

Alternate #5: I worry about her most of all. Can she stand up under the pressure? Will she be able to make a judgment based on fact not emotion? Will she get the opportunity to make a judgment? Can she handle that? Time will only tell. But she has been invited on the Ensanada cruise at the end of the trial. Some of the others feel they will need her expertise to help decompress after the trial. I call it an attempt to head off Post Traumatic Stress Syndrome. I sure hope I can get the time off from work because these people could surely use my counseling skills!

LUZ SPEAKS OUT

It appears that Judge Riley has talked with the attorneys because the cat fighting has slowed down. So has the drama in the jury room. The two younger ladies on the jury were talking and sharing today. Several jurors commented that the tension has subsided. It might appear that Judge Riley doesn't have to do anything but sit and listen but there is a lot more to keeping everybody happy. He reminded us that if we thought we were tired, just remember that the attorneys have been at this case for the past two years and basically work this case twenty-four/seven. When put in perspective, it really sounds petty for us not to get along.

We have heard some very interesting testimony this week. The court has heard sixty-seven witnesses thus far and the trial has been going for six weeks. We heard testimony from the female officer that took aerial photos at the crime scene and also Black Canyon where the body of Megan was found. She did a good job of verifying what others have testified to regarding the investigation of the case and how evidence was handled.

Next, we heard Luz's sister, Elizabeth describe Vincent and Luz's dysfunctional relationship. She had encouraged Luz to end the relationship about six months after it began. Elizabeth stated that Vincent had seemed nice, polite, and a good guy when they first met him. Her account was that he and Luz began fighting within the first year but continued to see each other off and on for about three. So far everyone has agreed that they did not belong together. Vincent had gotten to the point where he threatened Luz's life, her kids lives, and his own. He even called her to dry-click a gun into the phone so she would be intimidated. He told her he would kill her and nobody would ever find her body. Elizabeth remembers in the summer of 2000, Luz had a black eye. When she confronted Vincent, he stated he was sorry but she had made him angry. Once he threatened that, "You will never see your sister again. I will shoot her in front of her kids. You will never find her." Elizabeth told Vincent she would do anything to keep Luz from him and that she was attempting to get Luz back with her ex-husband. They had several confrontations in the past and Elizabeth told him on one occasion that he reminded her of O.J. She stated she wouldn't be surprised if they found a dead body in his yard. Vincent just laughed. Vincent was described as obsessive and possessive. This story reads like a typical domestic violence tale; control, manipulation, intimidation, and violence.

On July 4th, 2001, Vincent attempted to reach Luz at her sister's house but Elizabeth would not put the calls through to her. He called about four times during the course of the afternoon and Elizabeth finally told him, "You are not going to spoil our day." Their family was celebrating a daughter going off to college.

Luz told the court that she had left her children in Vincent's care on numerous occasions. Once on Memorial weekend, she went to Mexico for a family vacation. She trusted Vincent with her children and testified that he had a good rapport with her Down's Syndrome boy, Andrew. But Luz' teenage daughter did not like Vincent. The reason was never revealed but I imagine it was due to the fact that she had to report him on numerous occasions for harassing her mother. Elizabeth described Vincent as, "having a temper like the devil himself." She stated that he was verbally abusive around others but became physically abusive when he and Luz were alone. Elizabeth testified that Vincent hit Luz, pulled her hair, threatened and manipulated her. She also said that Vincent was jealous of the time Luz spent with her kids. Elizabeth told the court that his response to being confronted regarding his behaviors usually was, "Sorry."

Next was Doctor Mason, an expert forensic pathologist. He gets paid $350.00 per hour retainer fee plus $1,500 for "being under fire" as he put it. He was very much on his game and seemed to frustrate Defense Attorney Quinn. He would not give into Quinn's theories, and at one point it appeared Quinn may have conceded that this physician and professional of 30+ years may know something more than he does. I couldn't believe Quinn's arrogance! He said, "Well, yes, that could be right." Both Prosecuting Attorneys rolled their eyes at the same time. Aside from all of Dr. Mason's experience in the field of forensics, he also has a fascination and expertise with military style weapons. He has performed over 1,000 autopsies and many on bodies of gun shot victims. He worked in Vietnam for a number of years and became very familiar with the AK-47 assault rifle. His tests to determine the path and velocity of the lead core bullet that went into Megan were very convincing. He shot through steel, laminated glass and a soggy wet phone book to determine the velocity, and what would happen to this type bullet after going through all three. "The phone book is much like the soft tissue of the human body as far as penetration," he explained. He felt that the bullet broke up partly in the car door; fragments went through the clothing and then into her abdomen. He further testified that the thin steel bullet cover broke away and left tiny fragments in the intestinal tissue, while the larger lead core and steel jacket pieces traveled on and lodged in the muscle tissue of the back. Their density and size would allow them to travel 7-8 inches deeper than the smaller, lighter fragments. He had a good solid explanation for why the bullet did not hit any major vessels and just missed the left kidney. These shells are usually hard enough to penetrate objects and go right through them. That is how they got their name, "armor-piercing" rounds. But in this case, he thought that the glass was solid enough to cause the bullet to start to break apart. He felt that Megan probably did not lose consciousness because the car was steered by a sharp left into the median, demonstrating some volitional movement. Dr. Mason speculated that Megan could have temporarily loss consciousness "due to the bodies' fight-or-flight reaction." This is the psychological reaction to being under stress. For instance, some people pass out when they see a needle during a blood draw. In about one to two minutes a person will regain consciousness. This happens when the level of the head and the heart are repositioned. Finally, I was glad that he addressed the fact that Megan was probably reaching for her cell phone. That is why there was blood on her purse and make-up bag. The cell phone was found on the right floorboard of the Sun Fire. The charges of kidnap and attempted rape hinge on whether Megan was alive after being shot. Dr. Mason testified that evidence supported that Megan had handled her purse and makeup bag.

Dr. Mason gave a window of fifteen minutes to forty-eight hours that Megan could have survived. Since there was no reason she would have bled to death, then the only other thing that would have killed her was infection setting in.

This occurs when the bowels are punctured, releasing toxic material into the internal organs. "Our bowels are about 25 % bacteria and a significant infection could take your life within two days without medical attention." Dr. Mason also agreed that the body was so decomposed that it did not lend itself to evidence of sexual molestation. Apparently, the fluids that are excreted after the body bloats, will destroy any protein components such as semen, sperm or vaginal fluids. But Dr. Mason did believe that the clothing or at least parts of the pants would have been at or near the body when it was found. This further implies that the capris were not on Megan when her body was dumped there. He stated to his knowledge, "there would always be some portion of clothing found, even after a year." He also did not give much credence to the bullet embolism theory (bullet fragment being washed down the veins) by stating, "it is extremely rare."

I hope Dr. Mason's testimony about the last bits of bullet fragment will put to rest Quinn's obsession with it. He seems to get so zeroed in on the details that he misses the big picture. Megan died in that canyon because Sanchez shot her. He admitted it. Sanchez did not allow her to get medical attention, which would have saved her life. Everything so far has confirmed it. So why does it matter if they did not retrieve every last bit of bullet? Does that make her any less dead? Dr. Mason clarified that he was a pathologist and that Dr. Facklar is a surgeon, who operates on live bodies. This makes their experience different. This seemed to be a gracious manner of validating the expert witness testimony of the Defense.

Last but certainly not least, Luz LaFarga testified. Our curiosity was finally being quenched. She was an attractive woman (some say she resembled Sandra Bullock) but appeared as vulnerable as a child. Sanchez perked up when she came into the courtroom. I thought, this explains why he was wearing a nice white dress shirt and tie. He was looking forward to seeing her. They made very little eye contact during her testimony but did look at each other at various times. She cast her eyes away from him while she spoke, at which time he was all ears and eyes. He was like a different person than we had seen previously, alert and visually aware. The whole thing is kind of sick and sad, very sad. Luz appeared to be a hostile witness for the prosecution. She gave very little information that had not already been given. Her testimony did not appear to clear up much of anything. Especially, why she continued to see Vincent. She told the court that he became violent and angry within the first year of their relationship. They broke up on a regular basis so she was unable to answer questions regarding specific arguments or fights they had. All of the experience had run together in her mind. She kept stating that she could not remember details. Also, she told the court that she had blocked out a lot of the experience because it was so upsetting. Luz did verify that Vincent had threatened her life on several occasions. She verified her sister's story that he had told her he would kill her, and during a phone call had dry-clicked a gun in the phone. Sanchez' attempts to intimidate her had worked because even now, with him locked-up, her voice trembled as she spoke. Luz broke down and cried several times. When Vincent saw how upset she was, he also held back tears. At the point when she told of his threat to kill her, he just hung his head down. She admitted that Vincent was possessive and obsessed with her but she felt that he needed her because she could calm him down. That was her explanation for meeting to talk with him even after she had gotten a restraining order against him. What good the restraining order did is anybody's guess since she continued to see him, receive his calls and even had him sleep over. Through past Grand Jury testimony, Luz had stated, "she suspected Vince had killed Megan once she learned that he had raped those other woman." It wasn't until he was arrested that she learned about the rapes but Vincent still lied about how many woman he had raped. He told her only five or six. I felt sorry for Luz. I could only imagine how she might feel knowing that someone she lived with, left her children with, and made love to could do such things. She did not appear to be comfortable with the jury either. At times she looked over at us, but it seemed that she was afraid we were judging her. Today wasn't even the hard part. Starting Monday, she is expected to testify the majority of the day.

LUZ RETURNS

This is the seventh week of the trial and the first witness this week was Luz. She is returning to continue her testimony of last week. It was somewhat painful to watch and listen last week to the Prosecution attempting to get information from her. It was hard to determine if she was attempting to be helpful but not remembering, or if she was being oppositional. Many of her answers were, "I don't know" or "I can't remember." She testified all of Monday and seemed to do better with the cross-examination of Defense Attorney Helfrich. I felt that maybe Luz was torn between wanting to tell the truth and being afraid she would say something that would really hurt her friend, Sanchez. She did admit that she cared a lot for him and they had many good times together during their tumultuous relationship. Luz had the support of her sister Mary and some friends in the courtroom today. This probably contributed to her appearing more stable and expressive. She would look toward them at times for reassurance, and smile. I question her past history of mental stability because of a few statements she made. During a tape-recorded phone call to Sanchez while in jail, she was upset and stated, "I am getting sick again." It was obvious that she was very distraught about hearing that Vincent had raped several women during the time they were seeing each other. He lied, of course, and said that it was when they were broken up. They began dating in May of 1998. His first known victim was in September of 1996. By March of 1998, he had a fourth victim. So there was about nine months that he did not assault. He also attempted to minimize his crimes by lying about the number of women involved. Luz had agreed to aid the police by calling Vincent and asking if he knew anything about the disappearance of Megan Barroso. Luz testified that she had a suspicion that he had something to do with this crime once she heard that he had sexually assaulted those other women. She was sick with anxiety and kept asking during this forty-minute call if he had ever molested any of her children. He kept repeating," You know I would never do that, I love those kids." She told him that she could not believe anything he said anymore. When the Prosecution asked Luz if she thought Vincent was a liar and a manipulator, the Defense objected loudly. It was disclosed in testimony that he had used his threats to kill himself as a mean of manipulating Luz. She had never seen any evidence of him attempting to carry out these threats. But he had carried out his threats to hurt her. He had physically abused her in the past and had threatened to kill her on numerous occasions. She was convinced that he would carry through on these threats. Vincent threatened to kill her and throw her body where nobody would ever find it. This is what he almost did with Megan's body. I say almost because it is a miracle that she was found. Her body was dumped into a steep ravine with thick brush and debris lying on top of it. The forensic scientist from the crime lab, who investigated at the Black Canyon site, testified that the body had about two feet of debris over the top of it and about twelve inches underneath the body. It was obvious that this was used as a dumpsite, since many old car parts were lying around also.

In my mind, it appears that Vincent has been rehearsing his crime for some time now. Like he told his friend, George, he "felt like just opening fire on someone with the AK-47 and that he could dump a body and nobody would ever find it." He also had gone four wheeling in the canyon and was familiar with the area. Another interesting point is that one of the detectives told Luz that Megan resembled her. So if Sanchez hurts women when he is angry with Luz, do they also look like Luz? He was angry that July fourth weekend. Megan was probably just an opportunity presenting itself. Vincent was cruising the area of the 118 freeway that night near where Luz was partying at her sister's house and Megan was leaving a friend's house about the same time. But I digress.

Luz testified that she had told Vincent that he needed to get help for his anger problem. She also encouraged him to continue taking his medication that was prescribed through Mental Health Services. He did go to one counseling session in Simi that Luz was sure of. She had accompanied him there. But when asked if he followed through on his treatment, she was not sure. He told her he was still going but later it was indicated that he had gone to the DUI classes. He had received two Driving Under the Influence charges since Luz knew him. On one occasion, he turned the vehicle over, abandoned it and later reported it stolen. Luz would also try to get Vincent not to drink because she had seen evidence of his behavior when he did. On one occasion in July 1999, he was a best man in a friend's wedding and got upset with Luz for wanting to leave the party early. He created such a scene that the police had to be called. The police put Luz in a cab and sent her home. Due to their many fights and scenes, Luz's oldest daughter did not like Vincent. She had called the police on various occasions when her mother was being threatened by him. I found myself wondering if that was the only reason that her daughter did not like him. This was the typical domestic violence scene; female calls police to report abuse, then recounts charges, feels sorry for him, takes him back, only to be abused again. I believe that Luz could identify with Sanchez, maybe due to her own mental state or poor self image. She does appear to have very poor ego strength. But then again, we did not see her before this man traumatized her.

Things are not simple. One might ask, why does a woman like Luz stay with a man like Vincent? It seems that she felt he needed her. He would allow her to calm him down on many occasions. Just getting to see her would help him. He was totally obsessed with her. He also used emotional blackmail to keep her. She testified he was very good with her son, Andrew. She was a single mom with four children and he helped pick the kids up at school, watched them when she was away, and "gave" her his Suburban so she would have a bigger vehicle for her family. But Vincent also had a dark heart. Luz had allowed him to photograph her in nude poses and even some of their sexual encounters. But she did become angry with him when she found that he had video taped her on one occasion without her consent. It was impossible to determine if his story about not raping anyone while they were together was true because they broke up so many times. Luz could not re-construct dates. He did spend the night with her on July second, and then killed Megan on the fifth of July. He had one last assault on a female around July tenth before he was arrested on July twenty-sixth for stolen property. During his incarceration, the story began to unravel and the eleven women who had been sexually assaulted were all linked to him due to DNA evidence and some by the video tapings he had made. Vincent was sitting in Ventura County Jail with sixty-two charges against him when they also charged him with the murder of Megan. His story to Luz was, "they are going to try to put everything off on me now."

Luz had lived in Ojai since July 1998. Previously, she lived in the Simi Valley area. Luz and two of her children lived with Vincent at the Woodrow residence for a short time. But he became very possessive and jealous. She testified that he was not drinking at the time, but was still violent toward her. When Vincent got angry, he would blame Luz, stating, "It was your fault I got mad." Numerous phone calls had been made to the Ojai police because Vincent was stalking, coming to Luz's house uninvited, and attempting to break in. On one occasion, he came with a sword. A few times, he would stand outside and throw rocks at her window and yell. Telephone records would later reveal that he called her as many as sixty-two times in one twenty-four hour period.

When Luz inquired about him committing the rapes while they were together, Vincent stated, "Only when you were mad at me." This appears to be an effort to put the responsibility on her and not where it belongs. When asked what she and Vincent had in common, she replied, "We are both neat and detailed." Vincent was helpful and did nice things for her and her family. They enjoyed camping trips, trips to Disneyland, and family gatherings.

By November of 2000, Sanchez was threatening to kill Luz and himself. In January 2001, Luz caught Vincent peeking through her living room window while she had a male guest over. Anthony was preparing to go back to military duty in early January, when he found a note on his car. Vincent was apologizing for his behavior and giving his possessions to Anthony. This appeared to be a suicide note, alarming Anthony. He contacted Ventura Mental Health to admit Vincent. Anthony also informed Mental Health professionals that Vincent had threatened Luz and had access to a gun. For this reason, Mental Health considered him a danger to himself and others, and likely to carry out this threat. By law, they are required to file a Tarasoff warning. Mental

Health personnel notified Luz of eminent danger due to his obsession with her. After eight days, he told authorities that the shotgun was hid in some bushes near Luz' job site where the police retrieved the weapon.

Luz stated that Vincent was better and acting "normal" once he was placed on medication. They continued to see each other until the spring of 2001, making a ski trip in May. In June, Vincent showed up at the graduation party of Luz' daughter and made a scene because the ex-husband was there. Vincent had been drinking and attempted to pick a fight with him. The incident was squashed, and Vincent was allowed to sleep over because he was too drunk to drive. Luz testified that she was not sure if Vincent was still taking his medication, but felt that he was starting to get worse by June 2001. By July 2001, he had assaulted his twelfth and thirteenth victims.

When Luz got her Ford Ranger back from Vincent, she asked him about the rearview mirror being broken off. He told her that he had accidentally hit it with his golf clubs when he and Anthony were preparing to go golfing.

RED FAERY DUST

Tuesday was spent hearing the details of trace evidence from Dr. Jones, another forensic scientist in the crime lab. He testified that the collision marks on the Sun Fire and the Ford Ranger match up. He scraped minute particles off both vehicles, as well as cuttings from the truck and car seats. Blood evidence supported that Megan had been in the Ford Ranger. Defense Attorney, Quinn painstakingly attempted to establish if Megan was voluntarily moving by the time she was placed in the truck. Also the question of struggle was discussed in great length. Dr. Jones did feel that evidence indicated that she made several planned movements while in her car, one to pick up the make-up bag and unzip it and one to open her purse. The cell phone, which was found on the right floorboard was not blood stained however. Speculation was that she was reaching for it before her car stopped on the median of New Los Angeles Avenue. He did not believe that there was heavy bleeding to her right hand or abdomen because all the blood droplets and stains only amounted to about a teaspoon of blood. He testified about projected bloodstains verses gravity droplets verses smears or swiped bloodstains. Basically it is just as it sounds;

projected means evidence that a person is moving and blood is flung through the air, gravity is just dropped, and smears are deposited by movement on a surface. Dr. Jones was very detailed and systematic and became frustrated with Quinn by the second morning of testimony. Quinn kept jumping from one subject of evidence to another and back again. This caused Dr. Jones to shift gears a lot. He voiced his annoyance by questioning, "Oh, so what are we talking about now?" This appears to be a tactic of Quinn's. I can't believe that he would be that haphazard without motive. The DNA blood evidence matched Megan's as well as the glitter that was found in the truck and truck bed. (Her girl friend had sprinkled red glitter on everyone the night of the July fourth party). Dr. Jones collected thirty pieces of trace evidence, including ten particles of red glitter, and the victim's hair retrieved from tape lifts off her jacket. He testified at great length about his testing of the glitter. Through lighting and cutting tests, exposing the side layers, measuring the size, and doing chemical analysis, Dr. Jones found this glitter to be identical to the remaining bottle of glitter produced by Megan's friend who had sprinkled glitter on everyone that night. The details of this case are staggering!

The Sun Fire exterior was also examined and paint scrapings, tape lifts, and collision damage were reviewed. Exterior damage to the Ford Ranger was measured and matched. The right bumper guard had been recently removed. Also, Dr. Jones testified that there was a large ding to the right side, rear wheel. A plastic piece that was wedged in the door of the Sun Fire was consistent with plastic found on his truck. The purchase of a new bumper guard was used for demonstrating how it would have mounted on the truck. The damaged guard was never found. Sanchez' DNA profile was consistent with the DNA evidence found on many of the other assault victims. Dr. Jones pulled the story together but he could not say if there was a struggle in the Truck by reviewing bloodstains. Nobody mentioned that the rearview mirror could have been kicked loose during a struggle. If I were Megan and could not use my injured hand, I would attempt to kick my assailant. There has been testimony to the fact that the mirror would need sufficient force to break loose from the windshield and take part of the glass with it. Defense Attorney Quinn inquired about any evidence of a struggle inside the Ranger. "If there was a struggle in the truck, it would require speed and a larger area of blood deposits. There was no blood on the headliner, indicating that movement may have lasted only a matter of minutes," responded Dr. Jones.

Visual and chemical comparisons were made of the dirt on the license plate and it was believed to be "over-whelmingly similar." Chemicals were also produced on the paint pigment, as well as wax of buffing compound found in the crack of the Sun Fire license plate. Dr. Jones believed that this came from the Ford Ranger during the side-by-side collision. His testimony left very little doubt that Megan and Sanchez had collided on the roadway that night.

At least ten bloodstains were found in the Sun Fire. There was projected blood on the back of her make-up bag, blood smears on the zipper opening, lipstick case, and on the strap of her purse. Dr. Jones testified that these were due to handling. The car floorboard had cast-off bloodstains that were flung as Megan moved her injured right hand. Her green jacket had minimal bloodstains on the right inside sleeve, indicating that she did not have it on for long after her injury. Dr. Jones demonstrated how the blood could have been deposited, as the jacket was turned inside out while being taken off her body.

During re-direct, Prosecutor Corona established that all the bloodstains in the Ranger had been cleaned except one on the gearshift boot. Absence of blood spots inside the roof of the truck did not rule out Megan was alive in the truck. "If she had continued to bleed, it would have likely deposited onto the pants she was wearing. The wound from her right hand would probably not still be bleeding, as an injury such as this will start to heal within minutes," responded Dr. Jones.

The Defense's premise that Megan may have used cocaine that night was rejected after tests were done on a white substance found in a baggy in her purse. Dr. Jones stated that after observing it under a microscope, it was found to be, "a vegetable cell material, such as seeds or nuts. It looked like almonds."

Quinn, Defense Attorney objected to the complete testimony of the next two witnesses. They were two ladies that Megan had been having meetings with for several months. They established that they met near Gloria Drive for several months and Megan would go home around 7:00p.m. (Gloria Drive is the street where Luz' sister lives and Sanchez frequents). I felt that maybe the Prosecution was attempting to prove stalking of Megan prior to her death, but that did not materialize. Or maybe just to establish that Sanchez could have seen her before the night of his crime.

The Crime Lab Supervisor and expert in trace evidence and DNA, Michael Parigin gave details of his investigation in the removal of the body from the canyon. They did some very painstaking work, removing debris one piece at a time. The reason for this was to locate any trace evidence such as, a bullet fragment, zippers from her pants, or any remains of the white capris. He and his assistant spent six hours in the canyon to extract Megan's body. He described the yard waste as being about twelve inches deep under her body and two feet deep over her. He also did the lab work on the panties, jacket, and t-shirt of Megan. First by cutting approximately eleven pieces from the panties, using a process of wetting it and allowing the wash from the material to drop onto a slide. Then looking at it under a microscope, he determined that there was no sperm or semen present on the panties. He did a similar process with the t-shirt. Her jacket also had cuttings taken and a chemical was added to the material and observed for reaction. No sperm was found on any of the materials or on the truck seats. Mr. Parigin added that cleaning chemicals would destroy semen.

Mr. Parigin proudly testified that since January of 1999, the Ventura County Crime Lab has been deemed expert at PCR testing for DNA analysis. He produced a DNA chart with analysis of victim's Becky, Joyce, Lorraine, and Ursula, and found matches to previously collected crime scene evidence. He stated that Vincent Sanchez could not be eliminated as the DNA donor in these cases.

THE CRIME SCENE

One day was spent being driven to the 118/23 interchange and viewing the crime scene. At first, I did not understand what we could possibly learn from this but I was later aware why the Prosecution had arranged it. I walked the full route of Megan's car from the time it left the off-ramp until it came to rest on the median and was surprised at just how far it really had gone. The Prosecution had the photo displays of the crime scene used in court to demonstrate their hypothesis. Being here helped to put real-life to the photos. My thoughts were that Megan had fainted and that is why the car stopped where it did. Otherwise, she could have continued on up the road and gotten away from Sanchez. This was a very somber event. The press was present, along with many police escorts. They had arranged to have the streets closed, giving us limited time at each site.

We also viewed the Sun Fire and the Ford Ranger parked next to each other in the courthouse parking lot. We were allowed to open doors and look under the hood but not to get into either vehicle. For our protection and the protection of the Judge and courtroom personnel, two Sheriff's snipers were stationed on the roof of the courthouse with automatic rifles. I tried to put myself in Megan's place in that car with the three bullet holes coming right through the front windshield. I would have ducked far to the right to avoid being hit by them, which is what the Prosecution depicted in their video re-enactment of her shooting.

Our last and most depressing stop was Black Canyon Road, where the body of Megan was dumped. They had a marker placed in the canyon where her body was found and a rope so we could propel ourselves down into the canyon. Only a few of the men attempted to go down, as the hillside was very fragile and would give way as they descended. It was apparent to me that Sanchez did not place her body there but dumped it. The bush was much more overgrown and dense than what the courtroom posters revealed. I found myself marveling that some 300 Search and Rescue workers climbed in and out of that canyon in their search for Megan. As we surveyed the area, I couldn't help but wonder if the homes on the other side of the hill could have had a view of the dumping. It seemed that any one of seven houses could possibly have a view of this spot. But not many people are awake in the wee hours of the morning to catch someone dumping things. It was obvious due to the number of auto parts and things down in the ravine that it has been used for dumping on many occasions, and the testimony from several of the Search and Rescue personnel verified that there was debris such as yard clippings and old car parts down there. If Sanchez covered Megan in yard debris, he probably thought she would never be found. I said a silent prayer for Megan's spirit while sitting there and viewing the site. I really want to believe that she did not die in that canyon, alone and cold. And scared.

REWARD FOR
THE RAPIST

The process is uncovering the layers of truth. The science of criminology is all in the details. We, as jurors have definitely heard details. Helen Griffin, forensic scientist testified this, the eighth week. She testified in great length about her examination of the panties found on Megan's body. She ran tests on the weave of the fabric, the stitching patterns, size, the elasticity of the waist and legs, color and style of the panties. Very meticulous details to determine if these panties were similar to three other pairs of thong type panties that were found in Megan's apartment. After much time and detail, Ms. Griffin surmised that the panties were similar to the ones Megan was wearing at the time of death. She further stated that if she had a pair of the same style in a small or large, she would be able to examine them further to really be sure what the degree of difference in sizes really were. The size found on Megan appeared to be medium. They were manufactured in the Philippines and the Prosecution had not gotten a response from the company or from the local distributors of the panties: Target, K-mart,

Penny's, or Kohl's. It is fascinating to know what lengths they will go trying to uncover the truth. At first, I found myself becoming very impatient with the attorneys about these types of details. But later I realized that the whole case hinges on the details. The Prosecution Investigator Haas joked about being the panty expert. It was his job to research thong panties all over Ventura County.

This week the Prosecution focused on the patterns of Sanchez. Several witnesses testified to his chasing Margy on the freeway, through Simi and attempting to run her off the road. (Margy is the stalking victim referred to in this trial. I will call her victim #13, even though she does not fall in that timeline of events). This victim had stated through previous testimony that Sanchez tried to hit her car at least six times during the chase but she managed to get into a parking lot where the police were known to hang out and reported the incident. Margy testified in the Pre-liminary hearing and the Grand Jury investigation but was not willing to do so in this trial. So they used her testimony from these hearings to bring the information forward. There was some indication that the Defense felt her testimony was not completely true. Innuendo was that maybe she had embellished the story once it was determined that the perpetrator was Sanchez, the Simi Valley Rapist. Defense Attorney, Quinn became irate and demanded to know who had initiated that theory. The Prosecution had one of their Deputy District Attorneys read the one hundred-page transcript as if Margy were present testifying. This was unexpected as I had never heard of this procedure being done before.

Margy's husband, Mark testified on his wife's behalf. She had elected not to come to court and was placed in contempt for her non-appearance. Mark testified about Margy's early morning call of October 1, 2000. He described her demeanor as "scared and frantic." Margy had stated that she had been chased all over Simi Valley by a man who drove with his lights off for about a mile, and tried to run her off the road. Margy worked at a local restaurant and got off work around 3:00 a.m. She was traveling near the 118/23 interchange when she realized that someone appeared to be following her. At first, she thought it was a drunk driver just trying to find his way home. But when he continued following her, sped up, got on her bumper, and at one point turn his lights off, she knew she was in trouble. She exited the freeway and he followed her on surface streets. Margy managed to elude him after going on and off the freeways, and finally found policemen in a parking lot. She had attempted to drive to the police station but did not think it was open. She began telling a policeman her story, when he had to leave for another call. The officer told Margy to meet him at the station, and when he returned he took her report. When asked how Margy was doing now, Mark stated she still is not comfortable driving at night.

On July 8, 2001, Mark and some friends went to pick Margy up after work. As they drove the 101 freeway and then took the 23 East, Margy noticed a white truck with a camper shell. It had a firemen's emblem on the back window and she realized it to be the same truck that had chased her back in October. Mark insisted that she drive up along side the truck and when she did, the friends in her car yelled profanities at the driver. He exited the freeway. Mark wrote down the license plate number and they called the police the next morning. But it was not until August 1, 2001, that they were aware who the perpetrator was. Margy saw an article in the newspaper, reporting Sanchez' arrest. The white truck was in the newspaper photograph and the license plate was showing. The issue of whether Margy changed or embellish her story once she realized she had been chased by the Simi Valley Rapist was never resolved through testimony.

Officer Arabian, the Simi Valley Policeman who took Margy's report on October 1, 2000, testified that she flagged him down in a parking lot and was visibly shaken. With rapid speech, she described a male hispanic driver, with short hair on the sides, long hair on top, who had followed her too close. She could see his face in the rear-view mirror because he was such a short distance behind her. She was unable to get away from him tailgating her and when she got off the freeway, he got off too. He turned his headlights off at one point, but continued to follow her. Officer Arabian stated he had gotten a call so he asked Margy to meet him at the police station later, and taped her interview. Margy re-enacted the chase scene by telling the officer which streets they turned on and how she finally got away from him. Officer Arabian stated that at this time Margy was still visibly shaken and needed to calm down.

Another unusual events this week, was Investigator Haas testifying to the evidence he had gathered from various witnesses during his search for facts in the case. He explained why the Prosecution did not have the details about the panty manufacturers, what Kimberly had said to him when he interview her, her state of mind, and the recovery of all of Megan's panties that happened to be in Kimberly's possession. He stated that he felt that it was an "unusual keepsake" but that Megan's mother had given all of her friends some of Megan's possessions. Kimberly had taken the packaged panties belonging to Megan and stored them in her garage. This issue has really blown this case wide open. The panties that Megan wore that evening could determine if Sanchez had her change into the thong panties, possibly molest her, before leaving her to die in the canyon. The questions being: if he did not try to sexually assault Megan, why would she be wearing different panties when her body was found? Why would search teams never find her white Capri pants? Was she wearing any pants when her body was dumped? These are crucial questions to this case.

I find myself wishing we could ask Mr. Sanchez what he thinks his punishment should be for his crimes. Did he attempt to rape Megan? He did kidnap her from her car and take her body to the canyon. He admitted to shooting her and left her for dead. If he didn't rape her, does that mean that he is any less guilty? We know of at least eleven women that he did assault and others that he attempted to assault. Also, there are victims on videotape of his peeping incidents that have not even been identified yet. Does anybody know if he attempted to harm them? Were these incidents reported? Peeping and laying in wait are crimes. Invading a person's privacy is a crime. Terrorizing a community is a crime. Sanchez appears to have had a steady pattern of crime over the past five years, at least. There may be other crimes that we don't know about. This is a man driven by his own urges. He actually attempted to report some guys walking around in his neighborhood, indicating that they were carrying a black bag and may be involved with the Simi Valley rapes. When asked about this later, Sanchez stated, "Well, he knew there was a reward for the rapist."

END OF THE
EIGHTH WEEK

Ventura County field evidence technician, David Sellers photographed the crime scene and the residence of Megan and Sanchez. Megan's green jacket was seen by several officers and the roommates when they first searched Sanchez' home but they did not know the significance of the jacket at the time. It had been placed in the chester-drawers at the side of his house, along with other "souvenirs" that were later found. The jacket had been taken from the drawer and dropped onto the ground, remaining there for some time. Officer Sellers also collected into evidence, a black duffle bag found in the downstairs closet, shotgun shells from under Sanchez' bed, and a phone bill in the name of George Lopez, the name Sanchez had been using to make phone calls. The duffle bag contained one pair of shorts, two pairs of earplugs, one pair of long pants, and twenty gauge shotgun shells. Mr. Sellers also photographed the remains of Megan at autopsy, along with items collected, such as her bracelet, ring, fingernail clippings and bullet fragments. His testimony was to enter these items into evidence.

Ballistics expert, Jim Roberts returned from his trip and was then cross-examined by the Defense. Roberts had used laser beams to demonstrate the line of fire of the six bullets that went into the Sun Fire and into Megan. He asked a female officer about the same size of Megan to sit in the car to measure the relationship of the bullets to her body when fired. One bullet went into the engine, believed to be an effort to stop the car. Two bullets went through the windshield, one past her left shoulder lodged in the trunk and the other through the glass and missing her head. One bullet glazed Megan's right hand at the steering wheel. One came through the car backseat window and through the car, believed to be the first shot that was fired at her on the roadway as Sanchez attempted to stop her. The fatal shot went through the driver's side door and lodged in her abdomen or bowels. Mr. Roberts testified that the safety glass is designed to shatter, which it did onto the car seats. Windshield glass is made to hold together and it did, leaving a view of where the bullets entered the car. Roberts suspected that the cleaning rod from the AK-47 fell onto the roadway during use. Tests have been done as to the time elapse before a bullet hits its target and allows for a 180-degree turn. This elapse time gives a victim time to change their position before being hit, which is apparently what Megan did.

Joaquin Fernandez, the father of George (Vincent's good friend) testified that he spent three to four hours with Vincent on the night of July fourth. They talked and drank more beers after the Woodrow party had ended, around 10:00 p.m. Joaquin estimated that Vincent consumed about six to eight beers while they talked. However, he did not think Vincent appeared to be drunk. He described Vincent as "talkative, social, friendly, but not angry." Joaquin guessed that they had drank between fourteen to eighteen beers in about four hours. Later, they went to Vincent's house to look at some re-model work that Vincent had done. Joaquin testified that he was interested in having Vincent do some work on his house. He observed Anthony's new BMW parked in the garage. Joaquin's testimony was mainly to establish how much alcohol Vincent had consumed on the night of July fourth. They drank until approximately 1:30 a.m.

Joaquin testified that on July fifth, he witnessed Vincent washing his green Ford Ranger at about 5:30 p.m. and waved to him.

Prosecution Investigator, David Williams, a 21-year policeman for the Ventura County Sheriff's Department whose background is in major crime, was questioned regarding what Kimberly had told him about the panties. Kimberly had clarified the type panties Megan was wearing from photographs in January 2003. Later, when the panties were discussed, she described them as "granny panties." On January 21, 2003, Kimberly delivered the packaged panties that had been given to her by Suzan Barroso, to the Prosecution team. At the time, the panties were spread out onto a table and Kimberly identified cotton bikini style as the type Megan had on when she saw her washing her clothing at the family B.B.Q. on the fourth. Kimberly also re-enacted the story of how she became aware of Megan's undergarments. Mr. Williams felt that Kimberly was credible with her story and tried intently to capture all the details. The Prosecution was attempting to prove that at the time Kimberly first gave her story, she did not know the significance of the panties. Because Kimberly did not tell her story exactly the same each time, the Defense was attempting to pock holes in it. My thoughts on this subject are, many times a person's story is told according to how the questions are asked. Also, I feel that if you tell a story in the exact words each time, it begins to sound rehearsed and is too set. Why would you do so, unless you had to remember it the same way? A lie has to be rehearsed so you don't get caught telling it.

Prosecution Investigator, Richard Haas testified again. This time he was asked about his recording of mileage in and around the crime scenes. He told us that it was six minutes to the nearest hospital from the Kunan exit (which leads to Black Canyon). There are two major hospitals in the area with signs posted. From Sycamore exit (exit to Sanchez' house), it is an 8.3-mile drive to Simi Valley Hospital or 9 miles on surface streets. This is very damaging evidence that Sanchez could have helped Megan live, if he wanted to. Black Canyon to Los Angeles Avenue is fifteen minutes and 14.8 miles. So it would have been shorter to take Megan to the hospital than to the canyon. I noted that when the Prosecution took us to Black Canyon, we stopped at a Fire station before going up into the canyon. Sanchez could have dropped her off there for medical care instead of dumping her body and leaving her to die.

This is the end of the eighth week of the trial and the Prosecution has rested.

After eighty witnesses and mountains of evidence. The final piece of evidence was a videotape of two officers trying to get Sanchez to say what he knew about the disappearance of Megan Barroso. It was ninety-nine pages of transcripted dialogue. He never did admit that he knew anything, just kept repeating, "Now you guys are going to try and pin everything that has happened on me." Sanchez likened himself to O.J. and other guys in the news being unjustly accused.

THE DEFENSE'
PRESENTATION

The Defense seems eager to begin their presentation of the case. Their first witness was the treating physician at Hillmont Behavioral Center in Ventura. Dr. Liebert (a psychiatrist in acute care and crisis intervention) was a consulting physician, who did contract work for various organizations that needed a psychiatrist for a limited term. Currently, he is working in Arizona but flew in to testify about Sanchez. He had begun treating him once the Crisis Team admitted him to the center in January 2001. Dr. Liebert's initial diagnosis was Intermittent Explosive Disorder, Adjustment Disorder (the adult version of Conduct Disorder in children), Substance Abuse, and Possible Head Injury from an industrial accident. He described Sanchez as having an inappropriate reaction to stress, and he was unable to rule out Post Traumatic Stress Syndrome. (The signs for PTSS are: experiencing a trauma, numbing of feelings, re-living the event over and over, and being hyper-vigilant). Dr. Liebert testified that Sanchez "was in denial and had no insight into his problems. He also tends to minimize everything." He admitted through cross

100

examination that he did not have time to truly treat Sanchez or make a more accurate diagnosis, as Sanchez checked out of the facility against medical advice. The only information the team had to go on was the history given by Sanchez, which was not very reliable. He brother, Anthony had tried to fill in the gaps but he really had not been around Sanchez much in the past few years. He was working in Libya at the Embassy. Anthony had taken a leave from his work when he found how distraught Vincent really was. He brought him to Mental Health because he had threatened to kill himself and Luz. Dr. Liebert and his team had taken the threats very seriously and had filed a Tarasoff warning to protect Luz. Anytime a person informs a medical worker that he plans to harm somebody and had the immediate means to do so, law requires the Tarasoff. Dr. Liebert testified that they had not found any evidence that Vincent was suicidal, only that he admitted to threatening suicide to get attention from Luz, and to manipulate her to take him back. Dr. Liebert did not know the full story of Vincent, described as "slightly paranoid and guarded." He felt that Vincent believed that he had an undo power or control to keep him locked up. So Vincent did not disclose much to him or his medical staff. Dr. Liebert did not know that Vincent had sexually assaulted numerous women, only that he had an obsession with his ex-girlfriend. He stated that Vincent did not have any insight into the fact that Luz was finished with him, and the medical team had the task of making him aware of it. Vincent had admitted his anger control problems and did try to address them during treatment sessions. Vincent seemed to believe that if he just took his medication and went to Anger Management, he would get Luz back. If she was so important to him, why did he not follow through with his treatment?

The Medical Team was in the process of getting a 5250 hold (14 day) on Vincent, because they knew he had a gun but would not disclose where he hid it. Vincent finally told his

101

brother where the gun was, and because he was a voluntary patient, signed himself out of the facility. He left just days before they were going to run psychological and neurological tests on him. Dr. Liebert was very sure that they could have uncovered much of Vincent's troubled behavior, if he had agreed to the testing. It was offered on an outpatient basis, but Vincent did not take advantage of the testing or any further treatment. He actually left without his medication and was called back by one of the nursing personnel. The medication was free to him, but he soon neglected to take it as well. The recommendation was made for Sanchez to attend Anger Management sessions but his participation was never verified. The Doctor described him as, "noncompliant to treatment." He continued to say that a person with these issues would easily require at least six months in treatment.

Much time was devoted to understanding the diagnosis of Intermittent Explosive Disorder. Dr. Liebert says that a person will just "go off, for what appears to be minimal reason. Also, these outbursts are spontaneous and no planning or premeditation is involved." The Prosecution jumped on that like white on rice. "Well, Dr. Liebert, if a person stalks his victims, films his victims, kidnaps his victims, sexually assaults his victims, and takes possessions for souvenirs, doesn't that show planning?" The doctor conceded. "But what about his Adjustment Disorder," Prosecutor Corona questioned. "Well, they all tie in together and create a dynamic of behavior," explained Dr. Liebert. What he did not say is, that many of these diagnoses are catchall labels that attempt to describe certain behaviors. The Mental Health team is required to give a diagnosis before starting treatment, so they use the one that sounds the most like the behavior that is exhibited. There was also some mention of Narcissistic Personality Disorder. In my opinion, this sounds more like Vincent Sanchez; a person who does not have regards for others feelings, is totally self-absorbed, wants only what makes him happy, and does not truly get attached to people. Vincent was attached to Luz in an obsessive way. He said he loved her and her children, but why did he try so hard to ruin the relationship? He seems more concerned with what he wants than whether he pleases Luz or not. Why did he not take advantage of the help when it was being offered? Was he afraid his real intentions—his real problems would be found out?

As far as the Substance Abuse problems, there was not much doubt that Vincent's drinking was a problem for him. He had already had two DUIs and had to go to traffic classes. Most everyone agrees that his behavior is worse when he drinks. His head injury was never really proven. The doctor relied on Vincent's word about an industrial accident. None of the test showed that a head injury was present, but Dr. Liebert felt that he still might have "a closed-head injury." He stated that many times an injury will occur but the patient denies any symptoms. We need to see more proof on this one! (An important point to note is that Sanchez was assaulting women in 1996, and his industrial accident did not occur until 1997.)

From what we had heard thus far, I feel that Sanchez has a Borderline Personality Disorder. Not that it is my job to second-guess the doctors, but the following factors describe seven of nine areas of his personality: (1) frantic efforts to avoid real or imagined abandonment. (2) A pattern of unstable and intense interpersonal relationships characterized by alternating between extremes of idealization and devaluation (3) identity disturbance: markedly and persistently unstable self-image or sense of self (4) impulsivity in at least two areas that are potentially self-damaging (e.g., spending, sex, substance abuse, reckless driving, binge eating) (5) Recurrent suicidal behavior, gestures or threats, or self-mutilating behavior (6) Affective instability due to a marked reactivity of mood (e.g., intense episodes of dysphoria, irritability, or anxiety usually lasting a few hours and only rarely more than a few days) (7) chronic feelings of emptiness (8) inappropriate intense anger or difficulty controlling anger (e.g., frequent displays of temper, constant anger, recurrent physical fights) (9) transient, stress-related paranoid ideation or severe dissociative symptoms.

Dr. Liebert's medication regime was designed to diffuse the intensity of emotions and help Sanchez to grieve the end of his relationship with Luz. By January 17, 2001 Vincent was "showing notable distress and was having trouble sleeping." Sanchez was on a 5150 (7 day hold) when he was admitted to Mental Health but once they began aware of his threat to kill his girlfriend, they pursued a 5250 (14 day hold). Vince Kelly, the social worker that managed his case, described him as, "having no insight or understanding of the gravity of his situation. He exhibited a macho attitude about disclosing his personal life." Dr. Liebert defined Sanchez as, "blindly intense" when dealing with Luz. A reference was made to the theory of Dr. Morrison, a prominent professional, who states that, "many offenders are not mentally ill. Just violent, just evil!" Time will tell which type of offender Sanchez is.

Both sides have been referring to a 352 motion that was made by the Defense and stipulated by the Prosecution. The Judge jokingly commented that it was one of the few things that both sides have agreed on, and if we wish to know more about it, we can research it in the Law Library. I attempted to do so, but to no avail. I later found out that it has to do with redundancy of evidence. The rule allows the attorneys to stipulate so there is no need to continue to introduce excessive testimony. I found myself wishing they would evoke this rule more often!

DOCTOR FACKLAR,
I PRESUME

Doctor Facklar was the much-anticipated expert witness that the Defense had hinted to a few weeks back. He is a Yale man, and a Forensic Surgeon. Meaning that he had been considered an expert in many courts for some time. He explains the evidence of anatomy of the human body. He has done many studies with the way weapons; such as M16 and AK-47 affect the body. These studies were done using 200-pound pigs, as they represent a close facsimile to the human body and how the tissue performs when wounded. Dr. Mason (the Prosecution's expert) had done the same tests using wet newsprint. Prosecutor Corona did as predicted, asked his fee for testifying. Facklar stated that he usually requests $250 per hour but because he plans to retire soon, he has increased it to $400. This comment gave everybody a chuckle. Dr. Facklar is a reconstructive surgeon and performed military medicine. His specialty is ballistics. Actually, he founded the Organization of Wound Ballistics.

Dr. Facklar attempted to answer many hypotheses about what might have happened in this case. He stated that he could not disagree with the Prosecution's expert, Dr. Mason or the pathologist, Dr. O'Halloran who did the autopsy on Megan's body. He was troubled by the one-fourth grain bullet fragment that was never found and speculated that it could have dropped into clothing, lodged in the body, or went on through and out the other side. "It could have lodged in the car door also, they just do not know because it was never found." He reviewed the theory of the fragment acting as an embolism and traveling out through the blood stream. "This theory is very rare and would have to take into consideration that the fragment would hit a vessel wall without going through it." He questioned if the bullet fragments that were found in her body, were even in their original position since entry. He stated that they may have "settled" as the body began to decay. Dr. Facklar speaks with Dr. Mason on a weekly basis regarding cases and they share information. He stated that they differ only in that he is speaking from a surgeon's point of view and Dr. Mason is a pathologist. He indicated that Mason has done more work on decomposed bodies.

The time of death was another speculation based on where the bullet hit. He felt that if the bullet had hit any other major organs or vessels, it would have possibly killed Megan within fifteen minutes. A person her size would lose about one and a half quarts of blood before going into shock. This would not occur unless the aorta had a large opening where blood would flow rapidly. He does not believe that it was likely the aorta was hit at all. If she did not bleed to death, the infection of bacteria in her internal cavity would progress within two days. Even then, the body has a mechanism to block the bacteria in one area of the body, much like when a person has a ruptured appendix. Dr. Facklar went as far as to say Megan might not have died at all, if her body was strong enough to fight infection and she was focused on survival rather than pain. He did not feel that she would have any pain if the loops of the bowels were the only organ hit. But she would start to have fever, sweating, and some pain from an infection if the wound went untreated. "Treatment could have saved her life."

When asked if he felt Megan lost consciousness or what causes a person to do so, he stated that fear, shock or blood loss can cause this. He explained that many people, especially in battle, lose consciousness only when they realize they had been shot. "This is a case of the mind telling the body, I have been shot." If Megan had gone unconscious at one point after being shot, he felt that she would have recovered in a few minutes. An interesting fact-- when one is hit by a bullet in the heart, you can still remain standing for approximately ten seconds. So he asserts, "This dispels many of the scenes we see on television and in the movies." He continued testifying that a large amount of blood does not typically spill immediately. The clothing usually absorbs the bleeding since it does not spurt out. Up to two gallons can be held in the internal cavity. Neuorgenic shock or rapid bleeding will impede consciousness by causing the blood pressure to drop. He stated, "One can't rule out the possibility that the blood vessel may have been severed." One comforting thing Dr. Facklar said was, "Generally there is no pain in this type of wound, except to the local area. If the bullet fragments struck a major organ or more than one organ, like the aorta, a large hole would cause rapid unconsciousness in a matter of minutes." However, he felt it was unlikely that the aorta or the left kidney was hit.

Dr. Facklar has also performed tests on the time lapse before a bullet reaches its' target. He stated that the reaction/ response time is approximately one-half second from when the bullet leaves the chamber. In many police cases, where they are accused of shooting a suspect in the back, this fact applies. The person being shot has time to turn the body 130 degree in that span of time. So if he was facing you at the time you pulled the trigger, he could now be turned to the side or back. This theory has solved many cases of police officers getting charged with shooting someone in the back. Dr. Facklar summarized his opinion in this case by stating, "This case is full of uncertainty. The bullet going through the car door decreases its' speed but the breaking up of the bullet increases the chance of more body damage because the bullet spreads out."

Another interesting witness today was Doctor Norm Fort, a Forensic Alcohol Specialist and Ventura County Criminologist for thirty years. His job entails training others in blood alcohol procedures, maintaining the accuracy of the equipment, and testifying as an expert in substance abuse matters. He explained that when a person starts to have a reaction to alcohol, first affected is the mental portion of the brain. The drinker will experience poor judgment, limited reasoning and processing problems. Next, the physical symptoms show through slowed speech, balance, and manner of walking. Usually a person who is very intoxicated will drive slower than normal and be very fixated on the task because one has to focus in order to perform the task of driving. Driving is a multi-task skill and these driving abilities break down the more alcohol is consumed. However, he did concede that the "practiced" drinker or more serious drinker can mask the signs and will have made some adaptation in performance before others become aware of the level of impairment. A heavy drinker can hide the physical signs but not usually the mental factors. Indicators that alcohol has been consumed are red, watery eyes, alcohol odor, change in speech to thick, slurred, or rapid. A change in demeanor will result in either angry or being unusually happy. This happens because alcohol depresses the central nervous system. While driving, one may see changes in speed, weaving, going to slow, driving with headlights off, turn signal on, unnecessary use of brakes, or failure to yield to a police officer when pursued. He also explained the concept of tolerance of a drinker. Many calculations of blood level affects were discussed and it was guessed that Sanchez had a blood alcohol level of .15-.20 the night of July fourth. This was considering he is 5'7", 140 pounds, male, having drank approximately 12, 12 oz. beers and one ale from 7 p.m. to 2 a.m. and eating some pizza around 9 p.m. In California, the legal limit for blood alcohol is .08 while driving. Blood levels are evaluated on height, weight, gender (females tend to less tolerant), type of alcohol drank, amount drank, time period of drinking (taking in consideration that the liver eliminated approximately one drink an hour) and if the person has eaten any food. Fatty foods are known to help absorb the alcohol. By Dr. Fort's calculations, Sanchez was impaired or intoxicated on the night and early morning of July fifth. He testified that one is impaired at .10-blood level and intoxicated at .15-.20. At .35-.40, a person can actually die from respiratory arrest. Another interesting factor is that alcohol is still being absorbed thirty minutes after it is consumed, and will give a higher reading. Food will digest in four hours and no longer be in the stomach. While an experienced drinker may not show any signs at .15 blood alcohol level, he is impaired. When an officer checks a driver suspected of drinking, he will test for the ability to track a horizontal plane. If the eyes bounce, this is a neurological indicator of substance impairment. The road test for a drunk driver is based on listening, remembering and being able to perform tasks.

CELEBRITY JUDGE

Judge Riley is a celebrity of sorts. His face has been splashed all over the news and T.V. this week, pending arrest of Andrew Luster. This is the date-rape guy who gave women drugs and raped them while they were unconscious. He was tried in Ventura County Court under Judge Riley but jumped bail and absconded to Puerto Vallarta, Mexico. A modern-day bounty hunter went down and captured him but got locked up with him. Apparently, in Mexico they view bounty hunting as kidnapping. The FBI had been tracking him and was alerted to his whereabouts. They brought Luster back to California. The Ventura County Sheriff's received him at Los Angeles Airport and transported him to Wasco State Prison, to begin serving his conviction of 126 years.

We are into the tenth week of the trial. The Defense has called sixteen witnesses thus far. Three more witnesses testified to seeing the Sun Fire in the intersection of 118/23 on the early morning of July 5, 2001. They did not shed any new information to the story that I could decipher. Obviously, I am not including every person who was called to the stand. Approximately eight persons have testified to seeing the Sun Fire on the median. But they gave varied information. Mainly, the testimony was given to affix a time of the shooting and abduction of Megan.

Three of Sanchez's past friends testified to his driving habits. Basically, he is an aggressive driver, weaves in and out of traffic and sometimes uses poor judgment. His brother-in-law told the court that basically, "he is a good driver." The important point that came from their testimony was, Sanchez was hotheaded and became aggressive with a guy who had flipped off his friend on the freeway. I guess the Defense may be working on the angle that he might have gotten into a traffic squabble with Megan on the night of the fourth, implying road rage instead of a stalking, assault incident.

A friend of Margy's, the victim who reported Sanchez for chasing her and trying to run her off the road, verified that Margy had told her the same story. She also told her that some 200 photos of Margy were found in Sanchez' possession. This was new information and not substantiated by any evidence. There appears to be some embellishment to Margy's story.

Two emergency room doctors testified to the care they had given two of the victims of Sanchez. Annette had felt that she did not get adequate care when she went into the emergency room the night she was attacked by Sanchez. After listening to the doctor who examined her, it was apparent that he did not hear the whole story of the assault. He was not aware that she had gotten hit over the head with a beer bottle. He stated he saw no evidence of injury to her head or any neurological damage. He did see bruising and a cut on her back, however. She complained of a tender elbow, which he gave follow-up care instructions for. His belief was that she would contact her own physician on Monday and follow through with any care that was required. It seems this is another case of not enough information given or the right questions asked. The doctor did not know of the choking incident, nor if Annette had lost consciousness. He knew about the bite, and commented that she needed a tetanus booster within 72 hours. The doctor stated that Annette did not indicate that she had a loose tooth. He said that Annette was very upset and the chaplain was called to comfort her. Annette was not given a neurological screening because the doctor saw no symptoms. Even though Annette had no concussion, the doctor saw her four more times that day. He did indicate that he did not have a complete story of her struggle with Sanchez that night but told the court that he assumed the police did. The doctor testified that Annette had a history of a cervical spine sprain and was offered a spinal collar, which she refused. When asked by the Prosecution if she showed any signs of confusion, the doctor stated, "in writing and verbally." He also explained, "emotions distort memory. Annette was very emotional at the time. Memory loss, problems with color, orientation, problems with eye-sight, may indicate that she suffered a concussion," the doctor concluded.

The emergency room doctor that treated Connie told how he had sutured two layers of a one-inch deep cut on her calf. The first to close the tissue and the other to close the skin layer. He was not aware that Connie felt that the chef's knife had gone clear through her calf and pinned her leg to the floor. He said there was no evident of this, as there was no exit wound on her outside leg. He did concede that, "Sometimes a victim might feel that their limb is immobile or pinned."

Ted Sebodoa, the father of Sanchez' friend, Peter testified that he has known Vincent since he was ten years old and had been neighbors. Vincent was the best man at Peter's wedding. The reason for his testimony was to verify one of the occasions when Vincent and Luz got into an argument and the police were called. Ted affirmed that there was beer and wine at the reception, and Vincent had been drinking. He did not notice that Vincent was unhappy until Luz arrived late to the party. Vincent's demeanor changed, and Luz and he began to argue. Mr. Sebodoa stated that this was the first time he had ever seen Vincent that angry. He was unable to calm him down and just grabbed him and held him. He was afraid that Vincent would hurt Luz. The argument lasted approximately 30-40 minutes, and since friends were unable to calm him, the police were called. Luz's version of that story was that she came late to the reception and did not feel well. Vincent was upset that she did not want to stay. Mr. Sebodoa testified that Vincent kicked her car and told her to "get the fuck out of there." Vincent had been drinking and Ted felt he was probably drunk. Ted was angry with Vincent for his outburst, and wanted the police to arrest him. He described the look on Vincent's face as, "the most violent, vicious look he had ever witnessed before." The Defense did not properly prepare Mr. Sebodoa before testimony, as the Prosecution had to keep objecting to his narrative testimony. He got confused and probably very frustrated with this. He became unsure when to answer and when not to. When Judge Riley dismissed for a recess, Ted left and did not return. The Judge and the Attorneys felt sure that he had just gotten confused and possibly thought he was through testifying.

Next, an Ojai Police Officer testified how he had responded on numerous occasions to Luz's residence, because Sanchez was harassing her. Sanchez would stalk her, hide in front of her place, throw rocks at her windows, or attempt to gain entry into her house by trying the doors. This officer became alarmed about this behavior, as he had just returned from a training program on how to spot stalking behavior. He felt that this was a true case of stalking and began to research the history of Sanchez' behavior through police reports. This system is called the Alert System, and logs all the calls made to a specific location. He discovered there were eight separate calls made to Luz's address regarding Vincent's obsessive behavior. The officer then advised Luz to get a restraining order against Vincent, which she later did. The policeman also tried to serve an Emergency Protection Order on Vincent, but could not find him to do so. Luz finally declined to press charges against Vincent because she was more preoccupied with her ex-husband at the time. Apparently, he had just gotten out of prison and was trying to get the children from Luz. At any rate, her plate was full and she felt that maybe Vincent would leave her alone after the restraining order.

Another of Sanchez' friends, Mike Perez testified regarding his driving habits. In 1987-1988, while on their way to the mountains, a car jumped behind Mike's girlfriend and Sanchez reacted by tailgating the guy. (Mike, the girlfriend and Sanchez were driving in three separate cars.) The guy flipped Sanchez off for tailgating. Then Sanchez decided to pull up along his left side and box him in. The guy then exited the freeway and Sanchez motioned for Mike to follow him. Mike gestured, "no." Mike also testified to seeing Sanchez race in and out of traffic and drive too fast. The Prosecution conceded that Sanchez has exhibited reckless driving habits, but would not label this as road-rage.

Ted Sebodoa returned to continue his testimony. This time, he seemed more prepared for what was expected of him. He briefly recounted the story of Sanchez at his son's wedding reception. Ted was angry with Vincent for making such a scene and felt the police should have arrested him. Ted affirmed he had seen Vincent drunk before and suspected that he had a problem with alcohol. He testified that he was so concerned for Vincent, that he made three attempts to contact him afterwards. Ted concluded, "Vincent was angry because being Peter's best man was one of the most important days of his life, and he wanted Luz with him." Luz had also been late to the reception because she had a sick kid and was talking with her ex-husband.

MORE EXPERTS

At this point, my mental health background is beginning to be helpful. It seems that many people associated with this case have some mental health issues. Nobody has testified to the mental state of Luz LaFarga but I had some questions the first day we observed her and heard her testify. At the time, she was very shaky and timid but I was not sure if that was strictly because she was so distraught about what her boyfriend had done. She did make a statement in her taped phone call to Sanchez regarding, "getting sick again." If not mental health issues, at the very least, poor choices. She had an ex-husband who was serving time in prison. Now she is testifying in a case where her boyfriend has threatened to kill her, as well as assaulted twelve other women and killed one.

Two psychiatrists who treated Sanchez at Hillmont Psychiatric Center (Ventura Mental Health) reported their impressions/findings of him. Dr. Kamson was the admitting physician. He based his opinions mostly on what the Psychiatric Technician on the Crisis Team discovered in the initial screening of Vincent. He knew that Sanchez had an unhealthy obsession for his girlfriend and had threatened to kill her and himself. Mental Health professionals are trained to take this information seriously. Because Vincent told them he had purchased a gun, wrote a note giving his brother all of his possessions, and had made these threats, Dr. Kamson considered him a harm to himself and others. Vincent was admitted on a 5150 hold, which allows mental health 72 hours to evaluate him. He was very volatile and angry when he arrived and expressed anger toward Dr. Kamson. For this reason, tranquilizers were ordered and were to be administered PRN (as needed) thereafter. Dr. Kamson testified that he considered Vincent an assault risk toward him, and possibly the treatment team. He also recommended a Tarasoff warning 1 & 2, as is required by law when someone threatens another persons' life and has the means to carry it out. Part one of the Tarasoff requires protection and part two is the warning to the potential victim. He testified that he was only the receiving physician and did not follow through on the Tarasoff. This was the responsibility of the In-coming Physician, who did follow up on this procedure. Both psychiatrists felt Vincent had significant problems that required hospitalization. But neither of them got to know much about the real Vincent Sanchez. They did not know that he had assaulted females, raped, stalked them or had stolen the gun from his roommate. They both testified that he had adjustment problems, anger problems and substance abuse problems. The history they received was largely from Sanchez, so they only got what he chose to share. Sanchez did admit to being depressed, having trouble with his anger and problems sleeping. Sanchez was diagnosed primarily with Adjustment Disorder and Alcohol Abuse, due to his depression and recent acting-out behaviors. After speaking with Anthony, Dr. Kamson learned that Sanchez was obsessed with Luz and on one occasion had experienced dry-heaves after seeing her with another man. He also was labeled Intermittent Explosive Disorder, due to his reactions to stress. Dr. Kamson and Dr. Leibert agreed that Sanchez needed medication for his moods. Dr. Kamson gave Vincent a GAF (global assessment functioning) score of 30. I questioned why so low, as did the Prosecuting Attorney. Dr. Kamson stated because he posed a danger to himself and others, plus was a substance abuser, and this made his score very low. My experience with the GAF is that a score that low is usually a person who is gravely disabled and not able to care for himself. The young females I work with at Youth Authority that are admitted with a psychiatric diagnosis: history of attempting suicide, unable to care for self, history of sexual, physical and emotional abuse will score that low. My point being that this screening is somewhat subjective. Prosecutor Dobroth summarizes by stating, "so if a homeless person who has a drinking problem were evaluated, he would get a score that low?" A final thought on this subject-- If most all the inmates in our prisons were evaluated for their mental states we would find that most all have Adjustment Conduct Disorders, Personality Disorders, Narcissist Disorders, Substance Abuse, or Anger Control problems. Does that justify their conduct? I say no. Unless a person is so gravely disabled that they do not know the difference between right and wrong, I feel we all have to be held responsible for our actions.

Kimberly's psychiatrist, Dr. Kassman was called to testify to her state of mind before and after Megan's death. He testified that he has been treating Kimberly for about ten years. She was diagnosed with Bi-Polar Disorder and Attention Deficit Disorder. To summarize these disorders: she has mood swings, depression, anxiety, and concentration problems. Her depression manifests itself in poor self-esteem; hating her looks and weight. Dr. Kassman explained that he treats her for the chemical imbalance in her brain and indicated another Psychologist treats her for grief issues and expressive counseling. His belief is that her mental health issues are chemically based and the behavior or precipitating factors are not the issue. "I treat the disease, not the feelings." Thank God she has a grief counselor to help her get through this! Kimberly was reported to be stable before Megan's death and then progressively began to deteriorate afterwards. She became depressed, hopeless, angry, stating, "I hate everyone!" At the time she felt responsible for the death of Megan. Kimberly felt that Megan would not be dead if she had not tried to return her cell phone that night. Kimberly had several hospitalizations following the death of her best friend, Megan. However, her psychiatrist felt that it was not the event that precipitated her regression, but her chemical imbalance. He did not concede when asked by the Prosecution, could an event such as this trigger a regression? He only stated, "she felt so." Well, from all I have learned in the field of mental health, what we think has almost everything to do with how we feel and then how we react to that. This is the theory behind Cognitive Behavior Therapy. Much success has been achieved by learning how to use these processes. I agreed with his comment of the need for a Bi-Polar individual to continue their medication regime. Going on and off medication does throw the body out of whack and makes recovery harder. Many persons with this disorder have managed to live very successful lives if they monitor their blood levels and continue to take their medication, provided they find a medication regime that balances their system. Dr. Kassman expressed concern when asked if Kimberly was taking street drugs along with her medication. He told the court that street drugs, "act as a steel umbrella, preventing the medication from completing its' full effect." When asked about her credibility, her doctor felt that she was competent and not anymore prone to lie or fabricate a story than you or I. He was concerned about her being required to testify in this case, thinking that the experience might set her back in her treatment. It seemed to me that Kimberly helping find out the truth about her friend might just be the most therapeutic thing that could happen for her. By giving her the opportunity to help verses feeling helpless and angry. I thought Kimberly demonstrated that she was making good progress when she testified in court. Her doctor stated that previously she had an obsession to talk with Megan's killer. Well, she was allowed to do so when she was in courtroom. It was a very tender moment when she looked at Sanchez and stated, "Vincent, I don't hate you. I don't like what you have done. I don't know if you raped her or not, but I sure hope you did not. I don't think Megan would hate you either." Sounded to me like a person who is on the mend and may be starting to forgive.

Dr. Kassman was asked about an incident that involved Kimberly hitting a parked car and not leaving a note. He did admit to writing a letter to the court on her behalf. His letter basically asked the court to consider her illness and state of confusion. Kimberly used the name of Prosecutor Dee Corona as a reference to her character. The Defense saw this as a clear indicator that Kimberly would use her condition to manipulate her way out of trouble. Kimberly later responded to this by stating, "Well, I felt close to Dee because I had talked with all of them so much. I felt they were my friends."

Dr. Kassman explained that ADHD (Attention Deficit, Hyperactivity Disorder) disrupts concentration and the ability to complete tasks. His physician's note on 7-3-01, described Kimberly as "growing competency," and he felt she had made significant improvement since the beginning of her treatment. After Megan's death on 7-23-01, he described her as "having anxiety, fatigue, excessive anger, feeling hopeless and having poor concentration." When asked about Kimberly's character, Dr. Kassman stated, "I can not comment on her character, just her disease." On 11-19-01, Dr. Kassman recalls meeting with Kimberly and her mother before hospitalizing Kimberly. He described her as, "self-angry, sad, agitated, wanting to die and having a plan to kill herself."

CREDENTIALS OR COMMON SENSE?

The Mental Health Psychiatrists have been well represented by the Defense testimony. I was hoping to hear from some of the line staff at Mental Health, who really worked with Sanchez and got to observe his behavior on a daily basis. My experience in the field, tells me that the Doctors have limited exposure to the patient and tend to rely on the information that is relayed to them by staff, such as the Psychiatric Technicians. Also, the Social Worker who managed his case, should have been called in to give details. The Defense seems to be impressed with witness credentials, and hopes that we will be also.

Vincent Sanchez told the Mental Health worker who screened him, that his father was an alcoholic and abused his mother. He also disclosed that he had a good childhood, was good in school and was being scouted in High School for a wrestling scholarship. His dreams were dashed when he got hit by a car on his motorcycle and ended up with steel rods in his legs. Vincent decided to quit school at this point.

He also told the professionals that he got into a lot of fights as a teen. His past has demonstrated that he is hotheaded. Several persons who grew up with Vincent testified that he had a temper and would "go off" on people, especially while driving. The Defense has presented this information so that possibly it will explain what happened on the night of July 5th, 2001. Their premise is that Vincent got upset with Megan on the roadway and just lost it. This story is not hard to believe, considering how he has operated in the past while driving. He was known to drive fast, weave in and out of traffic and actually chase people that pissed him off. On one occasion, he threw a tire iron at a car on the freeway because the guys had cruised in an off-road parking and sprayed water on him and his friends. There should be no doubt at this point to anybody listening, that Vincent is impulsive and hot-tempered.

I still am not convinced, however, that he has an Intermittent Explosive Disorder. That seems to me to imply that he has something neurological going on that he cannot control. The way that this disorder has been defined is, that he can just lose it at any time for no rime or reason. That does not appear to be the case. I guess it sounds as if I am second-guessing the doctors, but most all of his aggressive behavior has been explained by the actions of others, and then Vincent's reactions. However impulsive and reactionary he is, he felt he had just cause for his behavior. I feel that if the Defense wanted to stand on that diagnosis, they should have someone evaluate Vincent for this disorder with neurological testing. Also, they should have him evaluated for forensic predisposition. When the psychiatrist at Simi Valley Mental Health met with Vincent, he diagnosed him with Major Depression, and Mixed Personality Disorder. This seems to be the most accurate diagnosis to date. He has a substance abuse problem, anger control problems, is impulsive and exhibits anxiety. Vincent does not appear to have much regard for rules either. After driving drunk and getting one DUI, he got a second one. He wrecked a friend's vehicle one night while driving drunk and just walked away from it, later reporting it missing. My impression at this point is, that Vincent just does what he wants to do and worries about the consequences when, or if he gets caught.

Dr. Huemid, a psychiatrist at Simi Valley Mental Health was responsible for Vincent's treatment in February 2001. Ventura Mental Health had referred Vincent for follow-up care. The treating physician there changed his medication to address his depression and anxiety. Also, this was to assist him with restful sleep. He was taken off the medication that is given for psychosis, as this physician did not feel he had any. Dr. Huemid found Vincent's mental state to be, "Alert, responsive and well oriented. His memory was poor and he was not in total command of his emotions. Vincent was suspicious, not delusional. His insight and judgment were not currently impaired." Vincent was questioned about his drinking and he admitted that he did. Dr. Huemid diagnosed Vincent as Major Depression Recurrent. He was given another GAF and scored 46, based on his history and current social function. "Vincent was sleeping better, but still had low self-esteem." Dr. Huemid explained that Vincent's episode of drinking complicated his problems. Alcohol affects the central nervous system, impairs judgment and insight. It also adds to depression and agitation. Vincent had legal issues with his DUI and financial problems as well. Simi Valley administered his medication for three to four months, before he just stopped coming in. He also was referred to AA (Alcoholics Anonymous) and getting a Sponsor. It does not appear that he ever took advantage of this. He did receive some Anger Management therapy but we are not sure how much. My guess is, long enough to convince Luz that he is trying to get better. Vincent was described by the physician in March 2001, as "being in good shape." The last visit that Vincent kept with the doctor was in May and he was given a three-week supply of medication at that time. Dr. Huemid stated that his biggest concern with treating Sanchez was that he was continuing to drink along with his medication. He did convey to Vincent that this was not a good idea.

Vincent told Dr. Kaye, another Mental Health provider, that he quit school because of his motorcycle accident. He also admitted to having a fascination with guns, stating his father was a collector. He told Dr. Kaye that he had a head injury from a crane accident at the construction site where he worked for his dad. He reported that he got into a lot of fights and had been stabbed and shot before. Most of this was never verified by testimony. Dr. Kaye's three-hour evaluation of Sanchez, described him as, "crazy when drinking and overcome with emotions."

The last time Vincent picked up his medication was on May 17, 2001. Nobody knew just how much of the mental health services he had utilized. Dr. Huemid testified that he had access to services twenty-four/seven. Vincent had also been referred to Sierra Vista, a Simi Valley County Clinic for physical and medical care. Vincent was offered six free visits but did not return for their follow-up program.

JOGGING MEMORY

All the testimony thus far has stated Megan could have lived if she had gotten treatment within fifteen minutes. So did Sanchez have other plans for Megan? The only two people who knew the answer to that question are Vincent and Megan. Vincent won't say and Megan can't!

The Defense has been trying to determine if Mr. Haas gave Kimberly any information that would sway her testimony. For instance, the importance of the panties Megan was wearing that night. It is ironic that the young girl who felt the most responsible for Megan's death, would turn out to be one the more important witnesses in this case. Mr. Haas proved to be a very credible witness with his testimony. Most people cannot remember what they talked about yesterday but he recorded his conversations with Kimberly at each encounter. Not in great detail but to the extent of the general reason for the discussion and any thoughts that stood out in his mind at the time. Haas has worked for the District Attorneys' office for 23 years, and another nine as a Police Officer. So he has done his homework. He has a calm, deliberate and soft-spoken demeanor during his testimony.

Judge Riley jokingly stated he will allow the Defense to finish Haas' testimony before recessing for the day because he does not want him worrying about testifying over the weekend. Mr. Haas stated with a very dry wit, "I think I can get over it." It sure helps when the personnel use humor to break the tense in the courtroom.

Oscar, a young man and friend of Kimberly was called to testify about the events of July fourth. He had been given immunity when the Prosecution learned he was to be called by the Defense. He had helped Kimberly purchase cocaine on the fourth. The day before she planned to go up north with friends. There has been some holding back of the young witnesses in this case, because of their concerns about getting into trouble by law enforcement and/or their parents. Neither Kimberly nor Oscar would be specific where they got the coke or the name of the person who sold it to them. At this point, I am not clear what the significance of this testimony is unless it is an effort to impeach Kimberly again. We already know that she has used marijuana and cocaine in her past. But she testified that she did not use any this day. She had purchased it for their trip to Napa Valley to share with a friend. Oscar stated that it was offered to him but he did not use either. There was some variation in Oscar and Kimberly's story, but both said Megan was not aware of the transaction nor had anything to do with it. It seems that the Defense would like us to believe that Kimberly is a lying, drug-using manipulator.

The Defense recalled another of Kimberly's friends. She and her sister both testified to going to a beach party at Silver Strand the night of July fourth. They stated that a group of friends had sat on the beach and talked for a while. Apparently, there is some question if Kimberly and Megan wrestled on the beach, but I am not sure why this is important. The inference of sand has come up in past testimony but neither girl was aware of any wrestling that occurred on the beach that night.

Kimberly's mom was recalled to testify. Basically, the Defense asked her to bring the "sweat pants" that Megan had changed into while her white Capri's were drying. Two pair of "sweat-like" pants were brought in. One pair obviously was too large for Megan, but was taken from Kimberly's closet. The other pair was patterned pants with elastic waistband. These were the pants Kimberly identified as being the pants she gave Megan to change into. Kimberly's mother is very proud of Kimberly's memory for detail, and has acknowledged it to the court. It appears that the Defense is testing that very notion.

One of Vincent's roommates, Stephen Preuth and his girlfriend who stayed at Woodrow Avenue, were asked about their previous testimony regarding the night and early morning of July fourth and fifth. They had all partied together and watched fireworks in the front yard. Anthony had stayed the night and slept in Vincent's room. Vincent had a sleeping bag on the living room floor. Stephen stated that he got up to use the restroom around 2:00 a.m. and Vincent was not there. Nor was his green Ford Ranger. Stephen got up again at 4:00 a.m., while checking the house for locked doors, he saw Vincent washing his truck in the driveway. It was still dark outside. He remarked that this was not unusual but he did say something to his girlfriend about it. She stated that she knew for a fact that the time was 4:11 a.m. because she looked at the digital clock. Under cross-examination, Stephen began to waiver on his testimony. He stated, "he was ninety percent sure that it was the morning of July fifth, when he saw Vincent washing his truck. He stated that Vincent boasted about how good the truck looked after he had shampooed the upholstery. He also stated that Anthony did not spend the night there, but left around 9:00 p.m. on the fourth. I did not feel that Stephen was very reliable because he could not remember what he had testified to earlier. It was asked of him, that since he was Vince's friend and had helped him when he was not working, would he lie for him in this case. He insisted that he would not. When asked what Vincent's mood was like on the fourth, Stephen stated, "He seemed happy, not upset or depressed. He was hyper, as usual." He said Vincent was known for staying in his room most of the day and coming out at night.

After Vincent was arrested, he called Stephen and asked him to dispose of a trash bag in the recycle bin that had videotapes and photographs in it. He told Stephen that they were photos of Luz and he did not want others to see them. Stephen and Josh Reno became suspicious and viewed some of the videos. They then called the police. These were Vincent's sexual assault and peeping videos.

Jessica seemed to be a more credible witness than her boyfriend, Stephen. She had staying over on the fourth and woke up when Stephen got up. She recalls him telling her that Vincent was washing his truck, and checked the digital clock on the nightstand. The time was 4:11 a.m. Jessica has a three-year-old son, whom she takes to her mother's before going off to work. When she left the Woodrow residence at 6:30 a.m., she did not see Vincent there or his green truck. Jessica testified to noticing damage to the front of Vincent's truck at a later date and asked him about it. He told her that he had gotten boxed in traffic and got the dent. When Vincent was asked why he took Josh's AK-47, he stated he owed some guy money, but gave him the gun instead. On re-direct, it appears that there are some inconsistencies in her testimony, compared to the original transcript. But time does distort memory. Jessica seemed to be telling the truth, as she remembered it.

Kimberly was recalled to the stand by the Defense. She still looked like she was holding up pretty well. She was asked again about the sweat pants that she lent to Megan, the sale of the cocaine, and her accident with a parked car. Apparently, she had misjudged her space and hit a Porsche in the parking lot of a shopping mall. She stated, "A man began to yell at me and called me a bitch." She got out and looked at the car for damages and decided to leave a note. She stated she knew that he would check it after she left and see that it was a blank note. He did check the note and saw that it was blank. He left his business card with information for the car's owner to call him about the accident. The witness also took Kimberly's license plate number. When Kimberly did get contacted about the incident, she asked her treating physician to write a letter to the court on her behalf. Her psychiatrist wrote the letter and mentioned the names of Prosecutor Corona and Investigator Haas to vouch for her character. She referred to them as friends or persons who knew her well. When questioned about this, her reaction was, "Well, I did feel close to you because I was having numerous talks with you at that time and I felt you were very supportive of me." Every time she gets on the stand I feel myself getting very tender. I feel that she has probably suffered a lot after Megan's death due to her age, self-esteem, and volatile nature. It might sound like bunk to someone else, but I do believe her reaction to this question. I feel that this death has left her hanging on to any life raft that she can. However, I do think that she was hoping LA court would be understanding of what she was going through at the time, and to show her mercy. They did.

The man who witnessed Lindsey hitting the car and leaving the blank note testified. His story was the same, except that he stated he did not call out to her or talk to her at all. He was aware that she saw him, so he waited until she left then went up to the car to check the note.

There is yet another witness, talking about the 118/23-freeway exchange. He was Spanish-speaking and requested an interpreter. His name was recorded when the Simi Valley Police set up check-points during their search for Megan. They were passing flyers with her picture on it and asking had anyone gone through that intersection on or near the date of the crime. He fixed the time that he saw the Sun Fire to be 3:55-4:00 a.m. He saw the door on the driver's side open, the guard-panel lights were on, but nobody was in or near the car. He believed that a drunk-driver had abandoned the car. He did not stop, only slowed. It seems to me that if you asked fifty people the same question, they would give you a least ten different stories. So far, we have had varying degrees of this story according to the time, door open or closed, lights on or off, wipers running or not, and engine on or off. The consistencies have been that nobody was seen in or near the car, it was on the median, some lights were on, and nobody heard the radio.

The officer who assisted with the checkpoint reported that there were approximately seven witnesses who had some information regarding the scene the morning of July fifth. He stated that the police took data of the number of vehicles that went through the area of 118/23 between the times of 2:00 to 4:00 a.m. They estimated that an average of fifty cars might have traveled on the 23, and another 100 on the 118 freeway around that time.

The Ventura County Crime Specialist was brought back to the stand and questioned about the bag of Megan Barroso's panties. She answered affirmative to taking one pair of blue panties out of the bag and booking it separate of the others, then sending it on to the lab for testing. I suppose the significance of this testimony is to show the securing of crime scene evidence, as she had already stated in her earlier testimony how the panties were processed. Two chemical tests were done and microscopic exam for semen and sperm. Neither was found.

James Fontaine, a six-year friend of Vincent's recounted how Vincent had lost his temper, racing on the freeway, yelling, and throwing a tire iron at some guys who had squirted them with water. James described this behavior as, "one-upmanship." He also said that Vincent was a calm, safe driver, who never lost his temper on the roadway. He did recall however, that once at a party Vincent lost his temper and picked a fight with some guy but they were able to break it up. I wonder if some of these witnesses hear the irony in their statements?

The next two witnesses verified being in the car with Margy and her husband the night she spotted Sanchez' white Chevy truck on the freeway. (Sanchez had two trucks). As they pulled up to Sanchez, they began yelling profanities at him. Margy identified him as the guy who had chased her back in October of 2000. Sanchez exited the freeway, but not before they took down his license plate number.

Officer Neuman, a California Highway Patrolman, testified to stopping Sanchez on August 13, 2000, for speeding and weaving widely. His blood alcohol was .088 and he was arrested for unsafe driving. Officer Neuman reported him as, "agitated and uncooperative." Luz was with Sanchez and was also arrested for public intoxication.

Vincent's older brother, Frank testified regarding Vincent's driving habits. He said, "Vincent was very aggressive, scary at times, going in-and-out of traffic, tailgating, speeding and impatient." Frank got a chuckle from the courtroom when he stated, "I wanted to put on a crash helmet to ride with him." Most everyone has been consistent regarding Vincent's driving habits. He is reckless and shows poor impulse control.

Since the Prosecution had implied earlier that Megan and Luz had both lived in the La Club Apartments, possibility during the same span of time, the Defense asked the apartment manager to look back through old occupant records. She was unable to provide any evidence to support this premise, as her records only went back to October 1999. They may have been attempting to establish if Sanchez had seen Megan there.

The Simi Valley Police that met Connie (victim # 7) at the hospital the night of her attack testified that her demeanor was "docile and calm." When the officer interviewed Connie, she told him of the home invasion and robbery and stated their struggle had only lasted a few minutes. Officer Van Hock witnessed a two and a-half-inch laceration to Connie's right calf and felt that the scratches to her neck indicated injury resulting from the struggle. It wasn't until later that Officer Hock learned that Connie had lied about not being sexually assaulted. Connie told him that the suspect had been in her room for about an hour, rummaging through her jewelry, and that she had lay in bed for about an hour before calling the police for help.

PRENTKY IS PRESSURED

Dr. Prentky has studied the motivations and characteristics of the sexual offender, and classified the various types. He stated that Sanchez was the Power/Reassurance type. He described him as a non-sadistic rapist with a high degree of sexual drive. The motivation for rape falls into two categories: Power or Highly Sex-driven. Dr. Prentky does not see Sanchez raping just for the power of it but that he is driven by the urge for sex. He describes him as a man who only uses the power or violence necessary to get compliance from his victims. "This explains why he will later try to act as if his victims want him there, or treat the rape as if he and the victim are dating." Sanchez has asked several of his victims if they were enjoying the experience or if they want him to stay the night. This behavior was described as the fantasy element of his rapes. This is to say that he felt the victims would start to like him and want him to stay, or want to see him again. Dr. Prentky placed Sanchez in the 6-7 category, which is non-sadistic, but did say that some of his behaviors during the rapes could be classified as a 1 or 2, which is the opportunistic rapist. He does not see Sanchez so much in this category because of the pre-planning of most of his attacks. He describes him as having, "a high degree of rape fantasy." Factors that explain his high sex-driven crimes are: the pre-meditation of his crimes, the planning, stalking behaviors, videotaping the rapes for viewing later, and the taking of personal possessions of his victims. Dr. Prentky believes that Sanchez views the tapes later as a means of fulfilling his urges so he won't rape again. Explaining that once the tape does not bring the same arousal, then he goes for another victim. The doctor describes the violence used as instrumental violence, meaning only what is required to get the victim to do what he wants to complete the rape. It differs from a sadistic rapist, who uses more violence than is needed (known to be expressive-aggressive) during rape. When Sanchez comes up against resistance with a victim, he will exert the power needed to bring her back into his control. "The pattern changed somewhat over time," Prentky explains. "The first five victims that fought back were able to chase him away or he would give up and leave. But around the six or seventh victim, he had begun to use more power to overcome them."

Dr. Prentky talked in detail about the very troubling tape of Tonya (victim # 6). This was the young girl who told Sanchez she was a virgin and pleaded with him not to rape her. "Sanchez went from callousness to compassion for some of his victims, but we did not see much compassion in this case." She repeatedly told him how much it hurt and all he said was "if you will stop fighting me, it won't hurt so bad." He was very frustrated with Tonya, and very self-centered about getting what he wanted from her. "At the least, this rape demonstrated his impulsiveness and anti-social behavior," stated Prentky.

Dr. Prentky's interpretation of the patterns of the rapes and escalation of violence was very logical. The doctor's opinion was that by November of 2000, Sanchez was unraveling and becoming more determined. This was eight months before the murder of Megan. By his seventh victim, he was changing his method of operation and beginning to make personal threats on their lives. Prior, he made threats to hurt their family or pets to get compliance. By the time he got to his eighth and ninth victim, he was becoming more violent and combative. "This shows a deterioration in Sanchez or a spiraling down of his behavior," explained Prentky. "After the murder, he went back to his original pattern, except for the fact that he took his last victim off the roadway. He made an incompetent effort to reconcile the two urges of control and compassion." He raped his last victim, Donna just five days after he killed Megan. When asked if the death of Megan was sexually motivated, Dr. Prentky stated, "Past behavior is the best predictor of future behavior."

There was a great deal of difference in the rape tapes of Tonya and Connie. The fact that Connie gave in to the rape at one point and began to actively participate in it, made the doctor ponder what was going on. I admit I did too. He questioned what she meant when she said on the tape, "I think I am beginning to enjoy this." His comment infuriated Prosecutor Dobroth, and she came out swinging in her cross-examination. "Do you recall that Sanchez told her he would kill her if she did not cooperate, and that she better make it look good for the tape?" After all, he had already stabbed her with a chef's knife and would not let her get medical treatment. (I'm paraphrasing). Don't you think that he was violent with these victims? Dobroth held up the chef's knife and waved it in the air. She became very confrontal because she felt Dr. Prentky was minimizing the assault on Connie. "Connie felt her life depended on making it look good." In comparing the victim incidents, Dr. Prentky stated, "by the time Sanchez attacked Tonya, he was beginning to make more direct threats, and he caused extreme genital trauma. Sanchez attempted to get verbal compliance but soon resorted to physical violence when he became frustrated with Tonya. With Connie, he had a flash of compassion when he went to look for bandages for her leg." By the time he attacked Annette (the victim before Megan), he was showing signs of expressive aggression." The fact that Megan showed resistance to Sanchez by not stopping her car, lead the doctor to state, "everything that night was expressive aggression." Prentky felt the motive for stopping Megan was rage. Dobroth probed, "Can anybody predict what another person is going to do? Is it not a fact, that Michael Kelly, a high profile rapist was released by your institution and raped and killed another victim in a short period of time?" Dr. Prentky summarized by saying, "that it is a very complex thing, and the more we learn about it, we can revise our findings. We can not always predict human behavior." When asked if Sanchez would likely re-offend, Prentky stated, "very likely. His motivation has remained stable across time. He generally targets victim's that were home and sleeping. They would be less likely to defend themselves, than if awake." When asked if he felt Sanchez enjoyed the conquest, Dr. Prentky replied, "Only the defendant would know that. His calloused insentivity to his victims is more typical of an opportunistic rapist." Sanchez had his head down throughout this testimony, but he appeared to be listening quite intently as he ceased turning his papers or writing.

At one point, I felt sorry for the Doctor because he was asked to give his educated opinion based on limited facts. His report of the rapes was summarized by the Defense, not from actual police reports. Also, as he mentioned in his testimony, he did not have his childhood or adolescent history to make his decisions about Sanchez' personality adjustment. Dr. Prentky and his associates had devoted almost a year of their time to this case. He viewed the rape videos and reviewed Dr. Warren's evaluation (she was a member of his firm who had initially interviewed Sanchez). At this point, I became curious why no forensic evaluation was done on Sanchez. Also, why did they not ask for more background history from his family? When asked if he had any victims' reports, he replied, "victims need time to recover, so information is more coherent." He was putting his reputation on the line and exhibited some frustrated with the Prosecution's line of questioning. He repeatedly expressed that he felt **all** rape is violent and that he was not condoning any of Sanchez' behavior, just trying to explain it to the best of his ability. I do feel that he should have been more prepared for this line of questioning, and insisted on more specific information from which to base his opinions. He would be a bit naïve to think that the Defense was telling him all that he needed to know, or to think that the Prosecution would not attack his credibility on this issue.

THE WAR OF EXPERTS

The husband of Margy was again called to the stand. The Defense is attempting to impeach Margy on her past testimony. The Defense focused on what her husband knew about alledged photos of Margy that were found in Sanchez' possessions. He stated that he had spoke with his wife very little about this subject, other than to be aware that some photos were supposedly taken of their recent home, as well as the past one. Reportedly these photos were taken inside their backyard, some at the bank, and around their home. Margy obviously felt Sanchez was stalking her. But when one of the lead detectives was questioned about the photos of Margy and her husband, he knew nothing of any such photographs. Officer Galloway was one of the lead detectives in the Sanchez case, and stated that it would have only been common courtesy for other agencies that were working on the case to provide any relevant information to his team. He also reviewed the peeping tapes and found none of Margy. However, they did not feel at the time, that Margy's incident had anything to do with Sanchez or a serial rapist. As a matter of fact, they did not even treat the reporting of this incident as a crime. More like a nuisance.

But when Margy called them some time later and reported seeing the guy who attempted to run her off the road, she gave his license plate number. The task force did not even run the plates then. The number lay on Officer Galloway's desk for a time before he was aware of why it was there. Not until Margy called them again, did they proceed to put any connection to her case and the other assaults. It is very perplexing that the Defense is so adamant about Margy's testimony being wrong. It seems they think that she might have just jumped on the bandwagon when she heard that this was a high profile case. I suppose this happens at times. People wanting to be part of the drama. There is no doubt in my mind that she felt she was in danger the night that Sanchez chased her on the freeway. Especially when she later found out he was the rapist they had been searching for. We still do not know the reason she refused to appear in this trial. But after watching the way the attorneys go after witnesses, I can relate that she might not want to go through testifying again.

Annette (victim # 10) is another ring for the Defense to grab onto. They have attempted to dispute her testimony by way of the doctor who treated her, the officers who questioned her at the hospital, and the detectives who interviewed her later. Detective Galloway is trained at interviewing assault victims. When he interviewed Annette the second time, he got more details. The second interview is to follow up, get photos of the injuries if needed and determine if the victim can remember any information that was not already disclosed. Detective Galloway explained that many times a victim will remember other details after some time goes by. Usually they are so rattled by the incident that they forget to tell important details of the crime. Annette was distraught, excitable, and was complaining of pain the first evening the detective spoke with her. He stated that Annette did not look any worse the days following her attack, and she did not mention that Sanchez had hit her fifteen to twenty times in the face, while in her hallway. She did acknowledge Sanchez hit her with his fist once she began to fight him back. She had cuts and bruises to prove that. She also had a cut in the center of her back from hitting something on her way to the floor. Annette told Galloway, "She was doing better but still in pain." Officer Galloway took this to mean better both physically and emotionally. She complained of an injury to her elbow and stated she was hit in the head with a beer bottle several times before it broke. She told how Sanchez bound her ankles with plastic handcuffs and when Annette cried, Sanchez stated, "these are too tight, I'm not going to hurt you." When she got the bindings off her hands, she jumped up and began to fight him. Annette bite Sanchez' finger and he bite her back. She threw a picture frame at him at one point. She never mentioned that she had gone unconscious, only that she went limp when he was choking her. At this point Sanchez released her. When she recovered, she grabbed a metal lamp and pushed a desk in between them. Apparently, Annette feels that her memory loss is a result of this attack. Her injuries were deemed serious and Sanchez was charged with Great Bodily Harm. (I wondered if a civil suit was in the works.) Annette had also testified that Sanchez threatened to extort her using some photos that he took from her room. When asked by the Prosecution about protocol requiring follow-up pictures of the victim, the Officer responded, "To my knowledge that is only necessary in child abuse cases."

The Defense asked their Investigator, Annette Town to testify about the route of the chase of Margy. She and Mr. Quinn drove the route that Margy had testified about when she was chased by Sanchez. Quinn got their speed up to 80 M.P.H. at times, explaining that it was safe to do so because the traffic was light. Prosecutor Corona asked what the speed for the area was and Annette Town stated approximately 45 m.p.h. Mr. Quinn remarked that he was afraid that Ms. Corona was considering a citizens' arrest, to which everyone laughed heartily. Ms. Town also testified to the road conditions and alternate routes one might use. I truly did not see the point of this. The fact still stands that he chased her, attempted to hit her car and frightened her. Sounds like a crime to me.

Next, a nurses' assistant from the Ventura County jail replied, "142 lbs," when asked what the weight of Vincent Sanchez was when he was booked into county jail. This information is being used to help coincide with the alcohol blood level testimony. This was the shortest testimony thus far. The Defense attempted to get this witness to speak about Sanchez having a history of suicide but the Prosecution objected, and the witness was dismissed. It is amazing just how much information is never substantiated but keeps getting carried forward! Nobody has verified that Sanchez ever attempted to kill himself. All anyone has is his word.

Carmen Sanchez, not related to Vincent except by the marriage of her sister to his Brother, testified to his driving habits. The Defense is really trying to make a case of road rage for Sanchez. He does show a lack of impulse control when dealing with others on the road. Carmen told of an incident when some lady cut them off on the freeway and Vincent got upset and tailgated her. He then got in front of her and slammed on his brakes and flashed his high beams on her. Carmen stated that the lady in the other car had done it first and Vincent just did the same back to her. Carmen was afraid because her young niece was in the car and cautioned Vincent to stop. He did, and that ended the incident.

Marc Taylor, a forensic scientist, who owns his own DNA Lab in Ventura, gave an explanation of how his lab went about testing an earplug found at the crime scene. The earplug was tested twice by two separate procedures, yielding no DNA of Sanchez. He also testified that through his years of research and testing of DNA, he felt that his lab could have found DNA on the panties of Megan. He stated that he knew of a few cases when a body was decomposed and DNA was still obtained from the clothing. When pressed on this issue, he was unable to site any specific case or provide any data on this opinion. He stated that he could however, go back through his database at the lab and pull up this information. It is interesting regarding how DNA is transferred: by handshake, through sexual contact, kissing, struggling, or by being in a living relationship. Factors that would determine the DNA of an individual would be the amount, contact conditions (such as environment), and bacterial activity. Dr. Taylor stated, "It is possible to breakdown DNA cells even if there is not enough to profile. He testified that sperm is composed of protein, and sperm cells are tougher than other cells, making them resistant to attack." This is contrary to earlier expert's testimony that decomposing liquids and bacteria will cause the cells to breakdown. This case is becoming the war of experts! Apparently, the Prosecution did not believe him because they did not request that he prove that. Also, I was left wondering that if he felt so sure that he could get DNA from Megan's clothing after a month, why did the Defense not ask him to do so? Why did the Defense not ask him to bring this data to court if they planned to have him testify about it? Much of the testimony that comes out in the Defenses' case seems to attempt to discredit the opposite side, rather than to prove their theories. But I suppose all they have to do is introduce doubt in the jurors' minds. When Dr. Taylor was asked if he ever testified for the Prosecution, "Yes, he replied a bit defensively, but they usually have their own government labs do their testing." Dr. Taylor admitted to testifying for the Defense at least one hundred times in the past. "Initial evidence is the most important part of determining what to go after. Ones' approach is critical," concluded Dr. Taylor.

Marc Firestone, another forensic expert and physicist, testified that he disagreed with Rusty Hague, the re-constructionist of the crime scene at 118/23. He has very impressive credentials; a Masters and Bachelors Degree in Psychics, worked in Forensic Engineering for forty years, and did nuclear research at NASA and for the Department of Defense. Also, he is an expert in vehicle crime and analysis of product defects. There seems to be some dispute about what happened first, the gunshots or the cars hitting each other. Mr. Firestone thinks that the area where the truck sideswiped the car would not have came in contact with the frayed bullet hole anyway. "Most likely, the gunshot occurred at the off-ramp and the possible collision was not on the freeway, but at the intersection." I say so what! The point is the bullet was shot into the car in an attempt to stop her or hit her. Who cares which happened first? He killed her, he shot at her six times, and she is dead now. That, in my mind, is the point! Mr. Firestone went on the say that he also disagreed with other points in Mr. Hague' scenario, and wanted to give other possible scenarios. The Prosecution seems tired at this point, and did not even want to humor him. Prosecutor Dobroth asked very challengingly, "So just what are your other possible scenarios?" This witness soon became disinterested in sharing in great length, as he did not get the reaction that was expected. I found myself wondering how much money do these experts get to just come and mess with our minds? I also believe they can tell when the jurors interest peaks or ebbs. I know mine was seriously ebbing at this point.

Sergeant Lorenzen lead the crime scene investigation, along with Officer Barrios. They did a taped interview with

Kimberly. At the time, there was no mention of the color, style, or type of panties Megan wore. On July 31, 2001, they re-interviewed Kimberly but still had no suspect. Kimberly was more open and told of the cocaine purchase the afternoon of July fourth. Her parents were not present during this interview. No issue was made of the cocaine or the panties at this time. Sgt. Lorenzen informed the court that the bed liner to Sanchez' truck had been removed for further inspection. This was while it was still at the Crime Lab. When the vehicle was later moved to an Oxnard Storage facility, the bed liner was set off to the side and got separated from the truck. Sgt. Lorenzen told the court that the case blew open on July 31, 2001, when they learned of the videotapes found at Sanchez' home. He then told Detective Galloway to talk with Josh Reno about his AK-47. A search warrant of the house at Woodrow uncovered a bag of knives, camera that was identified as Annette's, handcuffs, and miscellaneous papers. The green jacket of Megan's was observed on the ground near the desk where many of Sanchez' "treasures" were found. But it did not raise suspicion at the time, because it did not fit the profile of the other items that he had taken from his victims.

The Defense has now rested their case and the Prosecution can call rebuttal witnesses. It was so nice for the jury to hear that we had passed another milestone, signifying that we are getting closer to the completion of this trial. Those of us who are alternates are holding our breath, because we may be released as early as the end of next week. We are into twelve weeks at this and many of us have been here since the middle of April, during the start of jury selection. It is now the middle of July. It may sound that I have lost interest in the testimony at this point, but that is not true. I think many of us do not have patience for what appears to be useless information at this point, however.

PROSECUTION'S REBUTTAL

The Prosecution called only three rebuttal witnesses. The first witness was Mr. Lukas, who had traveled through a police checkpoint during the search for Megan. He takes the 118 at the 23 interchange on his way to work in Montebello each morning. He normally drives through that intersection about 3:55-4:00 a.m. but on the morning of July 5, 2001 he went through at approximately 2:55 a.m. He remembered this because he was going to his office to finish up some paperwork before going up north on a hunting trip. He always listens to the Howard Stern radio show that comes on at that time of morning. He testified that he saw the Sun Fire on the median with the driver's door open, the headlights on, and a shoe on the pavement outside. He also thought that he saw something that looked like a piece of cloth, either a small shirt or piece of bright cloth. He, like many others, thought that a drunk driver had left the car there or someone had run out of gas. Mr. Lukas did not hear the engine running, he was not sure if the radio was on in the Sun Fire or if the wiper blades were running. He stopped his truck about two feet away from the front of the car and attempted to look into the car. He did not see anybody in or around the car at that early morning hour. He did remember thinking that it was odd to see the shoe out on the ground, and wondered if someone was walking down the highway only wearing one shoe. He saw tail lights off in the distance. I wondered if that was Sanchez driving away with Megan. The window on the driver's side appeared to be broken because he remembered seeing some broken glass on the ground and around the window frame. This led him to believe that it was most likely a drunk driver who had occupied the vehicle. He testified that the windshield was also shattered, "like a rock or a bullet had hit it." Nobody asked him why he did not get out of his truck and investigate the scene more closely. I would have.

The police recorded all persons who had gone through the intersection on July fifth, and kept a log to refer to for their report and future follow-up. The purpose of the checkpoints were to investigate a missing person. The police conducted them on August second and third, from 2:00a.m. to 5:00 a.m. On August second, six persons stated they had seen the car in the intersection. On August third, one person saw the car. Some of these people were contacted later for further statements and others not. I suppose it depended on the notes that were recorded about what they had witnessed on that morning, because the police did not follow up on Mr. Lukas' statement. The officer who took notes at that checkpoint, only logged that Mr. Lukas reported, "abandoned car." Later in August Mr. Lukas was contacted by police when he returned from a short trip to Hawaii. Officer Ilano stated that his partner had logged the citizens' name, vehicle type, and license number, while he recorded what they saw the morning of July fifth. They also passed missing person flyers of Megan and the Sun Fire. Officer Ilano did verify that this witness had stated he went through the intersection about 2:55 a.m. that Thursday morning. After repeated testimony of various witnesses stating they had seen parts of the crime scene that morning, I realized the purpose was to establish accurate timeline. Did Sanchez have enough time to kidnap and possibly rape Megan, then dispose of the body, and get back to his house by the time witnesses at his home said they saw him? His brother, Anthony stated Sanchez was gone at 4:30 a.m. But his roommate, Stephen said that he saw him washing his truck in his driveway at 4:11 a.m. Due to the contradictions in testimony, it comes down to whom one believes.

David Williams, the Prosecution's Investigator appeared a lot more relaxed on his reappearance to the stand. I guessed he felt the case was going well at this point. Mr. Williams checked the police records to verify that Mr. Lukas had gone through the checkpoint, drove a GMC white truck, his license number, and the time he was logged in at the checkpoint. This information was entered into the court transcripts.

All the attorneys seem less pressured now. I can only imagine how relieved they must feel after all this time going through the minute details of this case and being this close to completion. After all, they had been on this case for two years; through the Preliminary hearing, the Grand Jury Investigation and now the trial. They can start to see light at the end of the tunnel. The Judge stated that we, the jury would get a few days away while the Attorneys prepare their closing arguments. He laughingly told us that we, "Would not want to be around them at this point." Tying it all together to make a cohesive picture, not leaving out anything important to their case but not being too redundant, would be their task now. And a very trying task I would amagine

Lastly, the Prosecution read into the court records the Preliminary hearing transcript of Vincent Sanchez discussing his use of a dart gun during his assault on Joyce (victim #5). Sanchez explained that a gun is more intimidating than a knife, which was his usual method of operation. He had taken the dart gun from his roommate, Josh again. No wonder Josh did not like this guy much! It appears that Sanchez just went in his room and took what he wanted. Sanchez minimized the incident of using the dart gun to scare his victim by stating, "I didn't even have the darts with me, and there were none in the gun." Another example of how his purpose is justified by his means.

CLOSING STATEMENTS

Week number thirteen brought a turn in events. Juror number eight was released and replaced by myself, alternate juror number five. What a difference a day makes! There was no explanation for his release but it did not come as a surprise to most of the jurors. He had expressed continued concern for the hardship that this lengthy trial was costing him and his family. My name was drawn at random by the court clerk. I was not apprehensive about the task, as I was motivated to see it through to completion. One juror asked me if I viewed things more seriously, now that I was a permanent juror. I replied that I only hoped I had taken good notes. He was the same juror who had jokingly asked me if they would be able to use my notes when I was released from the jury at deliberation time. I admit it is a sobering thought to have the weight of deciding the outcome of another persons' life. Being a person who has spent her life trying to teach and rehabilitate others, now I was being asked to ponder at what point does a person not merit another chance. Is Sanchez' life worth saving? How many of us could look a person in the eyes and tell them "your life is not?" Well, twelve people will soon be asked to do so. The attorneys are starting closing statements today and soon we will be reviewing some 500 pieces of evidence and going over the testimony of eighty Prosecution witnesses and forty-five Defense witnesses, plus three rebuttal witnesses. We have been at this task for over three months, and have now reached another milestone in the case.

In the morning, Judge Ken Riley gave jury instructions that took one and a half hours. It is a good thing that we will have copies with us when we go to deliberation. This is the first time that it has been spelled out just what all the charges are. Vincent Henry Sanchez has twelve felony counts against him. First Degree Murder of Megan Barroso tops the list, along with six Special Allegations. The Special Circumstances rule applies because of his past sexual crimes and there are two parts to them. The last two counts pertain to whether he intended to rape or kidnap Margy, and his use of a weapon (his truck) to do so. Now it becomes clear why the Defense tried so hard to discredit Margy's testimony. The Prosecution states that all the charges in this case are warranted. At the least, they feel that First Degree Murder, willful, deliberate and pre-meditated should be found to be true. Both sides agree that Sanchez did not set out to kill Megan but that the situation presented itself. At that point the Prosecution argues that everything he did from then on was willful and pre-meditated.

Prosecutor Dobroth did a good job of summarizing Sanchez' track record. She stated that "we should not get thrown off by all the smoke and mirrors, this case is simple, really." She laid it out in three questions: What was his intention? Why did he kill Megan? What did he do after he shot Megan?"

Another helpful exhibit was the timeline of his sex crimes. They began in 1996 with Becky, three more in 1997, one in 1998, two in 1999, and four in 2000, and his last two in 2001.

By now, we had heard the testimony of nine victims, but it had not been put into chronological order before. Sanchez did chase Margy and terrorize her, but who knows what his intentions were that night in October 2000.

Chief Prosecutor Dobroth reminded us that there was no proven history of suicide attempts of Vincent Sanchez, only his word that he wanted to by putting a gun in his mouth once. The Prosecution conceded that they also believe Vincent was not trying to kill Megan but to stop her. But if he did accidentally kill her, why did he not get her help to stay alive? Dobroth reminded us that he did not get help for Connie either, when he accidentally stabbed her in the calf. He certainly did not show any compassion for Tonya, the young virgin that he assaulted repeatedly. She also reminded us that he did make direct threats to many of his victims early on, not as the expert Prentky testified. Sanchez admitted to using a dart gun, "Because it was more intimidating than a knife." Dobroth blew holes in the Mental Health expert's testimony that Sanchez suffers from Intermittent Explosive Disorder. "He certainly does have a temper, anger control problems and is worse when he drinks." I was glad to hear her say this because I have felt all along that the Defense was trying to paint a picture of a person who can not control himself. If he was so explosive, why have we not observed any outbursts in the courtroom? A person who cannot control his impulses would surely have exploded with some of the happenings in the courtroom. Especially when Luz was in the room. Sanchez only hangs his head down and his ears turn red when his despicable behavior is described. Dobroth marveled at the fact that he was able to come home after dumping Megan's body in the canyon and go into a sound sleep. "His brother had to kick him in the foot to wake him up! Even after he did this murder, he did not show remorse. If he were suicidal, wouldn't he then try to take his own life? He had ample opportunity, and could have done it with a gun or with pills," Dobroth elaborated. The chief prosecutor exclaimed, "you do not need experts to tell you about Sanchez, this is just common sense."

"This case is not about Kimberly buying cocaine, her car accident, a guy named Oscar, or Kimberly's medical history, asserted Dobroth. This is about MEGAN!" By this time, Dobroth had built up to a fiery pitch and her eyes were flashing. She looked each one of us in the face and could barely contain herself when referring to, "this defendant!" Sanchez remained white in the face but his ears were red. She went on to say, "Much effort on the part of the Defense has been made to discredit Kimberly's testimony but that she knew nothing of the importance of Megan's panties until early 2003. She had already told her story numerous times before that. Nobody on the Prosecution had planted the thought or gave Kimberly information as to the significance of Megan's panties. We are talking about a very narrow window of time, stated Dobroth. Approximately fifteen minutes from the time that Sanchez shot Megan and pulled her from the car, before other cars drove through the area and saw a Sun Fire unattended on the median." She speculates that he had rehearsed the crime. The facts stack up like this: He had told two friends about "good places to dump a body." He went four-wheeling in the canyon and knew the area well. He cruised the 118/23 freeway regularly and knew the Newbury Park area because Luz' sister lived there. He knew the La Club Apartment area where Megan lived because Luz used to live there. He had access to an Ak-47 and was carrying it the night of July fourth. He talked to his friend, George about stopping a car with it, maybe shooting a cop, said he threatened once he started he would not stop. He was angry with Luz because she did not call him on the fourth. He was drinking and cruising around that night. He had tried to call Luz at her sister's house but she would not let him talk to Luz. He also knew that hospitals were near by but did not attempt to get Megan help once he shot her. Nor did he leave her body in the car so somebody else could find her and help her."

Dobroth pointed out that nobody could predict with uncertainty what another person will do. She repeated the testimony of Dr. Prentky to accentuate this. "Michael Kelly, a two-time rapist had been treated at Dr. Prentky's facility and was discharged as no longer a threat. After his release, he went on to rape and kill another victim. The Defense argues that Sanchez did not take victims off the highway. When in fact, two of his other victims were taken off the street. Megan was murder off the street!"

Prosecutor Corona, with calm conviction, recounted the medical experts testimony. "The coroner, Dr. O'Halloran speculated that Megan's survival time after the gunshot wound would have been up to fifteen minutes. Dr. Mason, the pathologist, stated she could have lived up to several hours. But Dr. Facklar, the surgeon for the Defense team stated she could have survived several days, as the body would began to protect itself from toxic infection."

Corona reviewed the timeline of events that July fourth evening. "Megan left Kimberly's house around 2:40 a.m., drove approximately fifteen minutes before she was called on Kimberly's cell phone and turned around to return it to her. Estimated time that shots were heard was 2:55- 3:00 a.m. Witness Lukas drove through the intersection and saw the abandoned car at about 2:55 a.m. He stated he had seen the taillights of a vehicle in the distance. Did he see Sanchez driving away with Megan's body? This is bearing in mind that people's clocks are five minutes or so out of sync."

Ms. Corona suggests, "that at the least, Sanchez is guilty of First Degree Murder with Special Allegation #2, Kidnap with the intent to rape. Special Circumstances Part #1,

Kidnap or attempted Kidnap to commit rape also applies." Dee Corona summarized Sanchez' behavior as, "capture, control, kidnap and rape."

DEFENSE CLOSING STATEMENTS

Chief Defense Attorney Quinn began his closing statement applying the Golden Rule. "Judge this case, within the law as instructed, as you would have others do you, impartially through reason and rule of law." He spoke humbly as he reviewed the rights of a Jury. He stated, "I bet you didn't even know you had rights." The goal of the court is to supply you with the facts in the case in a manner that assists you in reaching a verdict. We are to be treated with courtesy and respect. We have the right to expect that the attorneys will act in a professional manner with respect shown to one another, and the court. The court will explain in straightforward language and terminology. We do have the right to submit in written form, questions which will be shown to counsel to address or not address, as counsel deems necessary. We have the right to hear and understand intelligible questions and answers. We can expect the court to exercise reasonable control over the questioning of witnesses to make the testimony distinct and effective, to help determine the truth without wasting time. We have the right to take notes during the trial and have the court reporter read back any testimony of witnesses during deliberations. We are allowed to view any exhibits of evidence, as needed. Jury instructions must be read to us and written copies supplied during deliberations. The court strives to avoid delays, and to start the daily sessions on time in order to use our time efficiently. We are entitled to recesses during the day and the court will make efforts to accommodate juror's needs. Lastly, but not less, after the verdict is discharged, we have the right to discuss or not discuss the deliberation or verdict with anyone. Our identification is conditionally sealed and can be disclosed only on a showing of good cause.

As Quinn was speaking, a piece of silver flake floated down from the ceiling. Defense Attorney Helfrich looked up, and then to the bailiff to verify that someone else had seen it. She had a very perplexed look on her face. My thought was angels are among us and making their presence known. A complete sense of calm came over me.

Defense Attorney Quinn then began his attack on Margy's testimony. He repeated several times that she had chosen not to testify in this trial but had chosen to testimony in the preliminary hearing. He attempted to speculate why she did not testify, and to remain in contempt of court. "Maybe she got caught up in the fact that this was about a serial rapist. Maybe because she did not tell the same story at the Prelim that she told the police officer the first night Sanchez chased her. You heard a transcript of her telling Officer Arabian that Sanchez followed her through Simi but no mention of him trying to run her off the road." (I am paraphrasing). At the Prelim, she told the story of him trying to hit her with his truck five or six times. Was she too scared to come before the court again? Had they ripped her apart at the Prelim? After all, the idea that the Defense thought she was lying had been floated out there. Where did she hear this?

She might be feeling that she is damn lucky to be alive and does not want to face Sanchez in court! We were instructed that we could take her testimony as it stands but would not have the benefit of seeing her, or judging her demeanor. She also told several people that Sanchez had photos of her, her husband, their old home, new home, in her backyard, and at the bank. This implies that he may have been stalking her for a future rape. But the detective on the case, Sergeant Galloway was not aware of any photos of Margy. The jury was left with what to make of this. Had one of the detectives on this case told her about photos? We don't know where that story originated. Was it her imagination, as Quinn implied?

Quinn instructed us on the rules that govern the phrase, **Guilty Beyond a Reasonable Doubt**. He explained that this is the highest standard, void of emotion, passion, prejudice, partisanship, or influenced by the opinions of others. He stated that the attorneys are partisan, obviously. His team is for his client, and the Prosecution for the conviction of the defendant. But we, as jurors should not be attached to the outcome.

I felt it was valuable to go over this information with us. The attorneys have the difficult task of not knowing how much information we need, or how much is redundant. He apologized for not being sure just how much information to impart to us. I felt that he did not trust us, when I watched him cup his hands in almost a pleading motion. He stated that many of us probably thought we would enjoy a "vacation from our jobs but that this was probably harder than any of our jobs were. " He was right about that! Both sides have acknowledged the severity of the evidence we have had to view and hear, and expressed their appreciation for our patience and mindfulness. We have seen and heard things that many people will never in their lifetime be exposed to. But I have confidence that this group of people are strong and will be able to cope with it.

Quinn reviewed the charges and attempted to dispel many of them as, "just not logical." He stated, "When you apply a pattern of behavior of a defendant, you don't then go outside the pattern to prove a point. He argues that it was just not Sanchez' pattern to force females off the road for rape or kidnap, but rather his propensity for road rage." The Defense conceded that Sanchez was an accident waiting to happen, and that his behavior was escalating over time. But they also agreed that he did not set out to shoot Megan that night. Their story is that Vincent was angry that Luz had not called him that day because she was partying with her family (and her ex-husband was there). Vincent was very controlling and jealous and may have been stalking Luz at her sisters' home, when he ran into Megan on the roadway. Quinn also proceeded to describe a scenario where Sanchez shot Megan and then left the scene. Later, went back and took the body out of the car to destroy the evidence of his crime. He states that there was possibly an hour between the time of the shooting and when witnesses saw the empty car. The shooting had occurred around 2:55-3:00 a.m. and the last witness to go through the intersection before the police were notified was about 3:55-4:00 a.m. Some saw the driver's door closed and some saw it open. Quinn says that Sanchez may have gone back, took Megan, and left the door open. Testimony stated that Sanchez was back at his house by 4:11 a.m., washing his truck. This scenario does not seem to fly because all of the crime scene witnesses had one thing in common. From the first witness to the last, none had seen a body in the car. Quinn postulated that Mr. Lukas was just pulled in by the Prosecution last minute and gave two different times of morning that he was present in that intersection. This speculation did not jive with my memory or my notes. Lukas told the police 2:55 a.m. because he listens to Howard Stern and it was just coming on the radio. The officer had written on the log the morning of the roadblock that he came through at 3:55 a.m. Quinn's recount of facts were confusing because I remember this witness saying he went to work early that July fifth morning because of a trip he was taking up North. This practice should not be allowed, in my opinion. There is plenty of facts to ponder and remember without any of the attorneys changing them.

Quinn has postured all along that the piece of bullet not found, might have been enough to kill Megan. It is important to his case that she died soon after the shooting. Otherwise, we are left wondering what was done with her body before she was dumped. Whether Megan was sexually assaulted could mean the difference in what Special Circumstance applies. We are not to take into consideration the sentence when deciding the verdict in this case. That is one of the instructions that I remember hearing the Judge read. But it is very difficult to separate the two, crime and punishment. Usually, human instinct allows us to make that choice. How many times have you heard someone say, "Well, if he did it, he should fry." Or, "if she really did hurt those kids, she should go away forever." But using that logic just does not work in this case. Eighty-three pages of legal instructions to reach a just verdict govern us. I remember hearing other cases in the news that were confusing to me. Why did the jury have such a hard time reaching a verdict? We were soon to be a part of that very process.

Quinn assured us that the reason we were not seeing all the charges that Sanchez had faced, was because he had plead no contest (admitted guilt) to them. And the reason we were seeing these twelve charges was because he was not guilty of them. This was the sole reason we were in court and hearing this case. I really wanted to believe him but this just did not ring true. He instructed us to look at the factual issues: Who, why, when, where, and what. "We know Sanchez is

who. Why? To capture, kill or rape Megan? **When** was this decision made? **What** was his purpose for leaving his house with the AK-47? **Why** not use the AK-47 to accomplish the rape? It does not fit his pattern. **Where**? At the 118/23 interchange. **What** was the effect of the shooting? Death, to stop her, or render her unconscious?" My thoughts shift to the fact that we are trying to use logic with an illogical mind (Sanchez). Quinn pointed out that there were no modifying constraints to keep Vincent in check. He had been drinking and Luz was not available to him. He finished his argument with a story about the drunk who lost his keys in the alley but was crawling around on the ground, under a light post searching for them. A passerby asked him why he was searching there, if his car was parked in the alley. The drunk replied, the light is better here. This story accentuates that we not look for the easy answers but really go through the facts in this case. "Your beliefs should be based on facts, not feelings." I can understand his fears. After all, his team started out with an up-hill battle. Trying to make a convicted serial rapist believable or even likeable.

Quinn seemed very frustrated, as did the other attorneys when they finished their closing arguments. What else did he need to share with this jury to help us in make our decision? What could he say to influence our views to see it as the Defense did?

All the attorneys apologized for talking so long, going over information, even belaboring points. But they also knew that we were growing weary, as they were. We had already lost two original jurors in a week's time. One of the ladies had gotten pneumonia and bronchitis and asked to be dismissed. Number three alternate juror was called. I was proud when my speculation that he would be the next alternate selected came true. He laughingly accused me of being, "in the fix."

ATTORNEY HELFRICH'S CLOSING

Defense Attorney, Jan Helfrich was very concise, clear and confident with her closing argument. I enjoy her style because I am real clear on her interpretations. She began by giving a thorough explanation of Sanchez' pattern of sexual assault behaviors. The Defense had prepared a chart comparing all of his known victims and she reviewed it with the jury so we would understand the Defense views. She listed: his use of a mask to hide his identity, along with gloves and dark clothing. His attacks in the home, threats of harm to a third party, victim injuries, which ones were serious injuries but none lethal. He had taken jewelry and personal papers. He had filmed videos or still photographs, and his peeping demonstrated advanced planning. His concern for the victims' participation in the act and expressing some concern for their well-being. She asserted that he did not show any sadistic behaviors to any of his victims. These were described as the elements that were present in most or all of his sexual crimes. Helfrich went on to assert that he did **not** assault during the times when he and Luz were reportedly fighting. She cited the dates of police reports and stated there were no attempts to assault on or around these times. This struck me because I had remembered that he and Luz started their relationship in May of 1998, and he had only one known assault that year. It was in March of that year that he assaulted Lorraine. After comparing the dates of two of his crimes, I realized they were one month after he and Luz had experienced some very good times. One trip was a camping trip and the other was a family gathering for her dad's birthday. Sanchez told one investigator that he only offended when he and Luz were fighting. But the truth is, he had already assaulted four of his victims before starting a relationship with Luz.

Helfrich reminded us that the Prosecution had objected to much of Dr. Prentky's testimony regarding Sanchez' sexual behavior but that it should be noted that the Prosecution did not have a rebuttal witness to give a different opinion. The Defense also asserted that Dr. Prentky was supplied information to make an evaluation from both the Defense and the Prosecution. The Prosecution, who felt that the Defense had not given him complete or accurate information on which to base an informed decision, disputed this. I agree with that opinion. He had no childhood history, no adolescent history of adjustment or lack of, and the medical and suicide history was only what he had told and was not substantiated by any other source. Dr. Prentky protested that the sexual patterns were all that he was commenting on but acknowledged that it would have been helpful to have other information. In my opinion, this was what was lacking in many of the physician's evaluations. None of them had the whole picture of Sanchez. How he spent his days and nights, or his predatory behavior.

Attorney Helfrich attacked Kimberly's testimony and moral character. She charged that Kimberly was up north getting loaded on cocaine with her friends while the police searched for the body of her best friend. Question was made of why Kimberly did not come clean with the cocaine transaction even when it could have been part of the reason for Megan's disappearance. I felt that these comments were both unfair and not likely. There was really no reason to assume that Oscar going into a house on the fourth and purchasing cocaine for Kimberly had any thing to do with Megan. It was not even clear if she was in the car at the time, or back at the BBQ waiting for Kimberly and Oscar to return. The fact that Kimberly was inconsistent in her testimony could not be denied, however. Also, Margy created a problem for the jury because of inconsistencies in testimony. Attorney Helfrich advised us, " to use our collective memory to piece the facts together." I liked that because I knew that is exactly what it will take when deciding some of these issues.

In order to use –**disposition of behavior**- as a guide for deciding Sanchez' guilt or innocence, we could use circumstantial evidence but we have to apply the standard-**Beyond a reasonable doubt**. There is much circumstantial evidence in this case.

Ms. Helfrich stressed the Defense's position was Sanchez did not set out to kill Megan but that the shooting was expressed rage. She reminded us that his previous behaviors had been defined by Dr. Prentky as instrumental violence. **Expressed** violence is that he was impulsive and killed her in a fit of rage. **Instrumental** violence means that he used only the amount of violence necessary to get compliance. Wouldn't it be a shame if he shot her just to stop her car? Something went very wrong that night and we might never know just what or why.

Prentky's pattern of attack theory was reviewed by Jan Helfrich. Sanchez raped seven of his twelve victims. He kidnapped seven of twelve victims. He knew/selected eleven of twelve victims. He had peeping videos of four of twelve. He attacked ten of the twelve victims in their home. He showed advanced planning in all twelve crimes. No alcohol odor was noted by any of the victims. He wore a mask and dark clothing in nine of twelve incidences. He wore gloves in ten of his twelve crimes. He used restraints in three of twelve cases. A knife was his weapon of choice in eight of twelve attacks. He made threats of violence to get compliance in eleven of his twelve attacks. He threatened to harm a third person/pet in eight of twelve cases. He took one victim to his house for rape. He chose all white or Asian females. He used his own truck in three attacks (Donna, Margy and Megan).

Defense Attorney Quinn concluded closing statements by reviewing doctors O'Halloran and Mason's testimony regarding how long Megan could have lived. Then he brought up the issue of the remaining bullet fragments. Megan's consciousness, or lack of was rehashed. He closed by stating, "It would be an easy burden to lower the standard, when applying the facts to this case."

PROSECUTOR CORONA'S STATEMENT

The Prosecution is allowed a second rebuttal argument because the burden of proof lies on them.

Prosecutor Corona began by giving a comparison of Sanchez' crimes and demonstrated all of the things that were different about each one. As she went through them, she pointed out any differences and describes his behavior as "evolving." She demonstrated how he was adapting to each circumstance and learning from what did not work. "If it worked, he would repeat it. If he did not have good results, he tried something new the next time." There were as many inconsistencies to his crimes, as there were similarities. On one occasion he would run when confronted, and on others he stayed and exerted more control over his victim. If he could not control them on one occasion, the next time he might try handcuffing them. Early on, he would flee if challenged but later he began fighting back. He did not always use a mask, gloves, and rape kit. He did not always drive in his own vehicle or stay in the home during the assault. He did not videotape or photograph all of his victims. At least one occasion, he used a dart gun to contain his victim instead of a knife. He did make direct threats of harm to some of his early victims, contrary to what Dr. Prentky stated. So Dee Corona's summary is that he adapted to each situation and went from there, making her argument very compelling.

The Prosecution also advised us not to rule out all of Margy's testimony. Yes, there were some differences in her earlier story but those could be explained by her sheer terror the night she first reported the chase on the freeway. Her husband testified that she told him that night she was almost ran off the road by some guy. But it did not show up in the police report or in the Prelim testimony. "Margy's fear was very real," stated Ms. Corona. The car chase did not spark any real concern on the part of the police that night, even though the report was turned over to the crime task force. It still did not raise any eyebrows when Margy called back again around the July 10, 2001 and stated she had seen the guy's license plate number who had tried to run her off the road back in October of 2000. The license number was taken down and placed on the desk of one of the detectives, without any explanation. The police still did not respond to Margy's report. What finally got their attention is when Margy saw the photograph in the newspaper (July 30th) of the truck that Sanchez drove and the license number showing. Margy again called and told the police, "this is the guy who chased me and tried to run me off the road." At this point, the police started to draw a connection with the rest of his crimes. The weird part of this story is that Sanchez had been calling Luz continuously over the past few days. Sixty-five times according to his phone records. The night he chased Margy on the freeway and through Simi, he went home and called Luz about 3:08 a.m. This blows holes in his statement that he did not stalk other women when he and

Luz were involved with each other. Or was it because Luz would not see him?

"Mr. Lukas, the man who had gone through the intersection about 2:55 a.m. on the fifth of July, was very believable. Corona reminded us that he had spent more time at the crime scene than any other witness had. He stopped his truck, looked into the car, noticed the shoe on the pavement, and also a piece of cloth near the car. Nobody else had testified to seeing a piece of cloth." (Some of the jurors later speculated that it might have been the Capri pants, which could have later been picked up by Sanchez.) "He had very little time to remove the body from the car and leave before being seen. Lukas may also have seen his truck lights in the distance, leaving the scene." Mr. Lukas told the Prosecution that he had seen the driver's door open and some glass on the pavement. At the time, he thought that it was the result of a drunk driver accident that had left the scene, like everybody who had seen the Sun Fire that morning.

Prosecutor Dobroth spoke again about the remaining bullet fragments. She reminded us that Dr. Mason felt that there might have been many small pieces that spread out in a path, not one larger piece that was not accounted for. Her conjecture was that if there had been another large piece of bullet, it would have been found. After all, the forensic team spent six hours just removing the body from the canyon the day Megan was found. The forensic investigators' testified that they took each piece of yard debris off and looked through it as they uncovered Megan's body. When they got her uncovered, they placed a sheet under the edge of her remains so that nothing would fall when her body was picked up. They then wrapped the body in the sheet and placed it in the body bag to transport. It seemed highly unlikely that they would have missed any bullet fragments.

Dobroth attacked Mr. Quinn's story of the capri pants being taken off to wipe up any blood that may have been on Sanchez' truck or on his hands from handling the body. Quinn also postured that the white pants needed to be removed because it was a full moon that night and they just stood out too much. This story was much more reasonable. The fact that the pants were taken off at all was troubling to me. Myself, and many of the jurors later speculated that this was an indicator that there had been foul play. Dobroth asserted that she could not tell us where those white pants were, no more than she could tell us where the bumper strip from Sanchez' truck went. But she did assert that if we found one, we would probably find the other. She continued to say, "Crime is not always proven to a science. If it were, all we would have to do is put the data into a computer and let it spit out the results." What she did know, however was, " Megan did not deserve to die. She did not deserve to be kidnapped and raped. She did not deserve to have her body dumped in the ravine as if she were a piece of garbage." Hers' was a very strong and emotional argument.

Dobroth finished her argument by explaining the difference between first and second-degree murder. She made it clear that the Prosecution did not want a conviction on second degree. We later heard that Sanchez had attempted to plead guilty to second degree but that the Prosecution denied it, and wanted to push for first degree. She also reviewed the terms Special Allegations and Special Circumstances. She explained reasonable verses unreasonable doubt. She gave us some information on how to deal with circumstantial evidence. Dobroth told us that in the least, we should find Sanchez guilty on First-degree Murder, Special allegation #2, and Special Circumstance Part 1: Murder in the first degree, with kidnap and the intent to commit rape.

After five days of closing arguments, we were now sent to select a foreman for our jury. The lady chosen is a good choice because she is very calm, organized, and has skills in managing people. She was my choice from the beginning. Three women and one man also expressed interest in serving as foreman. Anyone of them could do the job. We have a very strong and capable jury.

DELIBERATION BEGINS

Getting started was a bit shaky because several people felt they had the best idea on just how to proceed. Some wanted to get right in and see what others thought. Some of us wanted to organize before getting into expressing opinions. Since the trial had gone on for three months already, several people were very impatient and wanted to move it along quickly. But it is a process. It is not a good idea to push to quickly because as we found out, some people just have to mull things over in their mind a bit. I suggested that we agree on rules of conduct: basic good communications. For example, don't talk over each other, let everyone be heard, if you get angry while expressing your views, take a cool down period to re-group. Some felt we did not need to spend time establishing guidelines, but these were some of the same people who violated these basic rules of communication on more than one occasion.

The first day, three of the men spent time getting all the evidence in order by categorizing it according to how it applied to the case. We had some five hundred pieces of evidence to consider! We elected a secretary to write all the felony counts on a display board. It wasn't until closing arguments that we really knew what all the charges were against Sanchez. They consisted of twelve felony counts.

Next, one of the men read all sixty-two sexual charges that Sanchez had plead guilty to. We had testimony of one hundred and twenty-six witnesses to refer to. A couple of jurors had numbered and dated each witness so we had easy reference back to their testimony. The bailiff requested that we view the weapons early on, so they could go back to be locked up. All other evidence would remain with us until we completed deliberation. Many of us began reading and making ourselves familiar with the eighty-three pages of jury instructions. Others began reviewing their witness testimony notes.

By the end of the first day, we agreed that we would start the next day by deciding on Count #11 and #12. These were the two lesser charges that involved the stalking of Margy. For this reason, we felt they would be easier to decide. But as we got into the discussion of evidence, this did not seem to be true. We struggled with them for almost two days. There was conflicting testimony regarding Margy, so our instructions were to go with who and what we believed to be most reasonable.

Everyone seemed to be relieved by the end of the first day. We had accomplished several needed tasks. I suggested a tentative agenda for each day so that we would stay focused and also feel a sense of accomplishment. I felt this was important because of the frustration level of deliberating. Many liked the idea but by the third day, we no longer needed it.

Some jurors expressed anxiety about too much preparation work. They felt we were wasting time organizing and "not getting to the job at hand." Personally, I felt that preparing and organizing makes the job easier because you save time in the long run. It seems logical to review rules and evidence prior to voicing our opinions about the case. But it really comes down to personal styles. Two of the jurors, who did not feel we needed to start by reading the jury instructions, took up time arguing about things that could have been resolved had they made themselves familiar with the instructions ahead of time. But all is well that ends well.

By the middle of the next day, everyone seemed to settle into the process and go with the flow. We concluded that we had worked well together the previous day and people did feel a sense of accomplishment. That said, we went round and round about Margy's story. Truth is never quite as clear-cut as one might suppose. We decided to review the first recorded report that was taken by Officer Arabian the night of the car chase. We read over her testimony and the various witnesses who also had given testimony regarding her story. Many did not feel Margy was very reliable but did feel that Sanchez chased her with the intent to do something to her. All agreed that the truck was used as a weapon against her. So in the afternoon, we took a straw vote to see how close or far we were from each other on Counts #11 and #12. We were close but not unanimous, so we continued to discuss this testimony. One of the jurors is the "show me" type. This was frustrating to many of us but also necessary. It forced us to explore our own views and express exactly why we felt the way we did. He apologized for being so difficult but we told him that we needed to challenge our views and all agree. I expressed that it is valuable because it allows everyone to realize that it is safe to oppose the majority. We voted several more times that day. By the end of the second day, we had a guilty verdict on both Count #11 and #12. We decided that we would let it rest, re-visit it if need-be, but start on Count #1 the following morning. This felony charge involved Megan's murder, and possible kidnap to commit rape.

DELIBERATIONS
CONCLUDE

Today, we started by reading the Jury instructions for First-degree Murder. Then we went over the rules for Second-degree Murder. Jurors gave various scenarios for what occurred the night of Megan's death and the early morning after. The scenarios that the attorneys provided were reasonable but as one of the jurors indicated, there were also other possibilities. I gave mine:

The night of July fourth, Vincent Sanchez was drinking and watching fireworks with his friends. However, he was very upset that Luz did not even call him that day. He knew she would be at her sister's party in Newbury Park, as the family was celebrating her daughter going off to college. Vincent knew he would not be invited because the ex-husband (father of the girl) would be there. Vincent had already made a scene at one of the family gatherings when he became upset that the ex-husband attended. Luz' sister, Elizabeth had already told Vincent that she wanted to get her sister and ex-husband back together. So when the party at Vincent's house breaks up, around 1:30 a.m., he goes to bed. But he cannot sleep because he is worrying about Luz. I think he put the AK-47 into his truck with the intent to scare Luz, or maybe even to shoot her ex-husband or sister. They were both perceived as a threat to him from having Luz. So he gets up after 2:30 a.m. and drives over to Elizabeth's house but their party is over, and all have gone home. While in route, Sanchez sees Megan, who is attempting to return a cell phone to her friend, Kimberly around 2:40 a.m. Sanchez and Megan have some type of vehicle incident on the roadway. Maybe she sideswipes him or he sideswipes her. Vincent is still legally drunk at the time. He tries to stop Megan's car by either hitting it with his truck or firing a shot into the back right door, but she does not stop for him, only speeds away (like Margy did). He goes on ahead of her and parks his truck off to the side at the 118/23 intersection, and lays in wait. (I feel he has seen her before because they both frequent the same area). Megan does not see his truck when she comes off the freeway and stops at the light at the bottom of the ramp. Vincent is out of his truck already and begins firing shots into the car engine, in order to disable it. He misses shooting her with the shots into the windshield because she is leaning over. I believe he was trying to stop the car but did not have control of the gun. Megan steps on the gas and speeds off but not before he shoots through the drivers' side door. A single bullet goes into Megan's left side. A bullet goes through the front windshield, hits the steering wheel and grazes her right hand. She reaches for her purse to find her cell phone, then her make-up bag but the phone is not there. One of her friends had put the phone back into the purse when Megan dropped it onto the ground at Kimberly's. It probably had already fallen onto the floorboard, and she reaches for it but cannot quite reach far enough. (It was later found on the floorboard passenger side and further away than the purse or make-up bag). She releases her seatbelt in an attempt to get to the phone so that is why the seatbelt clasp had blood on it. As she reaches for the phone with her right hand, she turns the wheel with her left hand, causing the car to make a sharp left. By this time she has started to feel weak from the shot to her abdomen and goes unconscious. The car coasts onto the median and stops. Sanchez is there and promptly pulls her from the car. The police dog did not locate her scent on the pavement because Sanchez carried her unconscious body from the car. As he did, one shoe dropped off onto the roadway. Sanchez seat belts Megan in his truck so that when she wakes up, she will be somewhat contained. He knew she was still alive at this point. He drove her somewhere, nobody knows where and attempted to rape her. (Maybe in the back of his truck. Blood and pixy dust were found in the bed liner). He removed her white capris and disposed of them, along with his bumper strip that was dented. He had access to three possible sites to get her medical attention, two hospitals within six to ten minutes away or the fire department on his way to Black Canyon. He made up his mind at this point that he would not let her live because he did not want to be caught. He took her to the canyon that he was familiar with and dumped her body off into the ravine. I believe Megan was still alive when he put her into that canyon because of the manner in which her body laid. She was found lying on her side with her arms around her face, as in a comfort position before sleep. Sanchez covered her body with yard debris to assure that it would not be found. I think he had time to do all this and still make it home by 4:00 a.m. Two witnesses stated he was washing his truck by 4:11 a.m. He was not observed sleeping in the living room when the roommate's girlfriend got up at 6:30 a.m. for work. I think this is when he may have gone back to the canyon, thinking the body needed covering. It was a full moon that night and could have shown down into the canyon. By 8:00 a.m., he is sound asleep. His brother, Anthony has to kick him to wake him. I believe that Sanchez did intentionally take Megan's jacket. Possibly, he used it to cover her while in the truck and then threw it in the truck bed when he dumped the body. He kept it as a souvenir along with the other things that he stashed in the dresser by the side of his house. He kept the jacket because he did not see any evidence of blood on it. The rest of her clothes did have blood on them so they had to be disposed of.

I feel strongly that Sanchez had rehearsed this crime. Taking all the conversations he had with friends and roommates. ("I can stop a car with this AK-47. I know where to dump a body where it will never be found. I'm going to just go off on the next person who crosses me.") All of the elements just fell into place that night. Why did he put a loaded AK-47 into his truck that night? I also explained my ideas about his criminal thinking errors. He <u>minimizes</u> his crimes; "only 5 or 6 rapes," or "I was drunk at the time." He <u>blames</u> others for his own behavior; "if Luz wouldn't fight with me, I would not do these things." He also suffers from the thinking error of <u>uniqueness</u>; I am so smart, I'll never get caught. "I can hide a body where nobody will ever find it." I believe it is no coincidence that the crimes he committed while drunk are the ones that got him caught. He was taking more risks and getting sloppy about it. Lastly, I think it is very significant that the Defense wanted to convince us that Sanchez suffers from mental illness but did not pursue the neurological evaluation of him to prove brain damage or Intermittent Explosive Disorder. They had him evaluated for his sexual crimes but stopped short of a forensic evaluation. Their expert witness, Dr. Prentky was qualified to do one. They just did not ask for it. If you could have evidence to prove brain damage, or rule out criminal behavior, why would you not ask for it and provide that information into court evidence?"

177

Most of us agreed on Steps 1, 2, 3 and 4 of First Degree Murder: that a murder had occurred, it was an unlawful death, that this murder was committed with malice (expressed or implied malice) of forethought, and that the murder was done during the commission or attempted commission of kidnap for the purpose of rape. We agreed that murder was committed with **implied** malice. Expressed malice is when murder is in a fit of rage. It was not a stretch to entertain that Sanchez had attempted to capture Megan that night for sexual purposes. Only two persons felt that he set out to kill her because he put a loaded AK-47 in his truck that night. The other, because he shot off rounds into her car. We spent a great deal of our time discussing his intent to commit murder verses that his capture plan had gone wrong. Then the pre-meditated murder became a problem for some of us. We read and re-read the jury instructions. **Willful** means **intended**. **Deliberate** means a plan was formed. And **pre-meditated** means it was thought out beforehand. The tricky part is that not a great deal of time has to transpire for pre-meditation. We discussed the willful act of not allowing medical care or taking her for medical care when he had three possible options. If he was stunned that he had fatally injured her, why did he not leave her in her car so a passer-by could help her? At one point, we decided to stop discussion of this topic and address some of the Special Allegations. The last hour of the day was spent trying to be clear on the Special Allegations. Many of us were frustrated and acknowledged that we should have stopped about an hour earlier. We agreed to sleep on it and began again the next day. Sleeping becomes hard because your mind will not let you stop thinking about the details. Some jurors admitted to having nightmares.

Over the five days of deliberation, we voted, discussed and re-voted many times. Basically, we were stuck on the **Intent to Kill**. None of us bought the story of a simple act of road-rage. Some of us felt Sanchez did not intent to kill Megan at first, but later changed his plan. By August fifth, by 3:00 p.m. we notified the bailiff that we had arrived at a verdict. (Ironically, the same day Megan's body was found two years ago). In a brief half-hour the Judge had everyone notified, and we were in the courtroom delivering our decision. Judge Riley read the eight counts, nine Special Allegations, and two Special Circumstances into the record. Defense Attorney Quinn requested that each one of the Jurors give a verbal response to the verdicts rendered. Jan Helfrich sat red-faced from the beginning of our entry into the courtroom. Quinn was quiet and sullen. Dobroth, Corona and Prosecutor's Investigator Haas were all very stern, showing no expression. Sanchez looked down or straight ahead, white-faced with his hands clasped in front of him. The courtroom was full of news people, cameramen, and family and friends for both sides. The verdicts read like this:

Count 1: First Degree Felony Murder- jurors all agreed.

Special Allegation #1: Murder during an attempted rape- jurors all agreed.

Special Allegation #2: A. Kidnap with the intent to rape- jurors all agreed.

Special Allegation #2: B. Kidnap with the intent to kill- jurors did not agreed.

Special Allegation #3: Willful, Deliberate, and Pre-meditated-jurors all agreed.

Special Allegation #4: Committed with the use of an assault rifle-jurors all agreed.

Count 1: Special Circumstance 1: Part 1: Kidnap or attempt kidnap to commit rape-jurors all agreed.

Count 1: Special Circumstance 1: Part 2: Kidnap or attempt kidnap with the specific intent to kill- jurors did not agreed.

Count 1: Special Circumstance 2: Murder during the commission of attempted rape-jurors all agreed.

Count 2: Kidnap with the intent to rape-jurors all agreed.

Special Allegation #5: Use of assault rifle-jurors all agreed.

Count 3: Attempted Kidnap to commit rape- did not apply, as we had found him guilty of kidnap (count 2).

Special Allegation #6: Use of assault rifle.

Count 4: Kidnap

Special Allegation #7: Use of assault rifle-jurors all agreed.

Count 5: Attempted Kidnap- did not apply, as we had found him guilty of kidnap (count 4). Special Allegation #8: Use of assault rifle.

Count 6: Attempted forcible rape- jurors all agreed.

Special Allegation #9: Use of assault rifle.

Count 11: (Regarding Margy) Attempted kidnap with the intent to rape-jurors all agreed.

Count 12: (Regarding Margy) Assault with deadly weapon (truck)–jurors all agreed.

The jury spent much time on Willful, Deliberate, and Pre-Meditated Murder. We also spent much more time on the evidence surrounding the Margy case than we had expected we would. It could not be proven when Megan died, or if she was sexually molested but our instructions told us we could rely on circumstantial evidence and inferred evidence if it is strong enough. Also, the disposition of the defendant can be considered. Not all the jurors believed the Steven Preu and Jessica Shelton testimony regarding the time frame of the evening in question, but we did feel Sanchez would have had time to do the crimes and return by 4:00 a.m. on July fifth. Bottom line, the testimony of Kimberly did not turn out to be the tiebreaker that everyone thought it would be. A few jurors stated they did not believe anything Kimberly said, but that her testimony did not matter in their decision. The fact that Megan's capris were off the body and never found was a big deciding factor. If Sanchez did not molest her, why would her pants be off?

Judge Riley thanked the jury for our time and diligence in determining the verdicts. He cautioned us not read the newspapers or discuss the case yet. He told us that the three remaining alternate jurors would be back on Monday to join us with the Opening Statements for the Sentencing Phase of this trial. The Deputies escorted us out of the courthouse through the basement, so the press would not attempt to talk with us.

At first, I did not know how I felt. Later, a sense of calm and rightness came over me. And even though my mind could not get around the actual concept of this defendant dying for his crimes, I did not have second thoughts about my decision about his guilt.

I believe your mind tells you that his death may never occur, with the appeal process and all. But our instructions were to not let that alter our decision of his guilt or innocence.

SENTENCING PHASE

As we have returned for the Sentencing Phase of this trial, many of the jurors have expressed that they are having trouble sleeping and are spending many hours going over the evidence in their minds. I can't even imagine the thoughts that go through the minds of the victim's in this case! Now we will begin to hear in the victim's own words just how they are coping at this point in their lives.

Opening Statements from Prosecutor Dobroth, told us we could consider all Aggravating Circumstances. These were described as: past crimes of sexual assault, crimes against Luz (stalking, threats, physical violence), Sanchez' crimes against Megan (kidnap, intent to rape, and murder) and his conviction at age 22 of Felony Corporal Injury to a Child. Just when we thought we had heard the worst of it, there appears to be more!

Sanchez had plead guilty to a Felony charge when he was 22 years old, and had spent six months in State Prison for Corporal Child Injury. At the time, he had an eighteen-year-old girlfriend and was living with her and her thirteen-month-old baby girl, named Curstain. His story when arrested was, that the baby had fallen off the kitchen counter while he was feeding her, hit her head and stopped breathing. Later, evidence proved that she had been hit in the head, had her hair pulled out, and was suffering weight loss. The mother, Dona and Sanchez were both arrested for Child Abuse and Injury. It just gets harder and harder to have any compassion for this man!

Dobroth informed us that we would hear from family members and friends about what the loss of Megan has meant to them. She requested that we listen to all the evidence, Aggravated and Mitigating evidence that the Defense will present. She stated, "This is the path he chose to take. And in the end, you should not give life, but death to Mr. Sanchez." Her voice was devoid of any emotion while she made her presentation. For this, Defense Attorney Quinn commented and thanked her for not making it an emotional plea to the Jury.

Defense Attorney, Quinn began by thanking us for our time and effort in this trial. He stated that even though the Defense did not agree with the entire verdict, they respected our decision. He told us that Sanchez was a "very complex man. He did some really hideous things but also had a kind, thoughtful side to him." Quinn stated, "This would be a moral decision and spelled out the Mitigating Circumstances as: the fact that he plead guilty to most of his crimes, his positive character traits (hardworking, kind, artistic, competitive, helpful, supported self at an early age, not involved in gangs, has adult peer and family support). Also, his Setbacks and Limitations: Sanchez had a predisposition to alcoholism, had low self-esteem, concrete thinking, cognitive distortions, physical injury, an anger problem, depression, Personality Disorder, Paraphilia Disorder, and low academic success." He went on to say that we would hear from a doctor who has much expertise regarding Paraphilia, and "that it is not a disorder that <u>any</u> person chooses." We should also consider Sanchez' childhood: poor role models, physical abuse in the home, father was an alcoholic, fear, depression, and that the family suffered from the "Rainy Day Syndrome." The father worked construction and had many days when the weather was bad, that he had no work. So he would stay home and drink, making the rest of the family miserable. On these days, the children would avoid coming home after school or hide from their father. But he did instill a strong work ethic, as demonstrated by Sanchez leaving home and supporting himself. He stated that all of the eight children left home at an early age. Lastly, he mentioned the mental and emotional disturbance that Sanchez displayed. He told us that doctors would attempt to address this issue again. We were advised to factor in Sanchez' difficulty conforming his conduct as a result of mental disease or effects of intoxication. Quinn told us that we will hear testimony from family and friends of Sanchez, who still care and support him. This is going to be equally as painful as the Prosecutions' story. I am a strong believer that nobody is all-bad. Sometimes this opinion leaves me in a stalemate.

PROSECUTION'S CASE, SENTENCING PHASE

The first witness called by the Prosecution was Lorraine's mother. She testified on Lorraine's behalf because her doctor said it would not be a good idea for Lorraine to be present. Lorraine did testify before the Grand Jury, but shortly afterwards stopped talking altogether. Lorraine was fifteen at the time Sanchez sexually assaulted her. The impact on her life was devastating. She had trouble sleeping, withdrew, dropped out of school, would not go anywhere by herself, got depressed and suicidal. Lorraine's mother insisted that she go to a doctor and get help. The doctor gave her medication to help her sleep and cope with her anxiety. The mother described her as "zombie-like and fearful." She had stopped many of the activities that she used to engage in: swimming in the ocean, running, and drawing. Lorraine would not go in the car unless she had her dog with her. Her mother testified this was because she knew she would not try to take her own life if the dog was with her. Lorraine was very attached to her dog and suffer further anguish when the dog was killed the following New Years' Eve. At one point, Lorraine left home and was reported missing. When she was found, she was laying on the grave of her dog, half frozen. She had been there over-night. The impact of this crime on her family was also very great. The six-year-old brother, who had been in the house the night of the rape, knew something was wrong but was not clear what had happened. He too became fearful and would not stay alone. The mother described him as "taking on the anxiety of the family." Lorraine got some relief while in therapy. She later got married and had a child, but her mother states she still suffers with shame and fear. She put up a wall around herself and began working excessively. She demonstrates problems communicating with her husband even now.

Suzan Barroso, Megan's mother testified next. She informed us that Megan was her first child, and described her as a beautiful, dainty child who loved to dance. Art and Suzan had divorced when Megan was around three. Megan had lived with the mother most of the time, except a few years while in High School. Megan loved Ventura County and when Suzan moved to Templeton, Megan swore that she would return to Ventura. She moved in with the Ester family for two years so she could stay in the area. Megan was active in Irish dance and clogging from the time she was five years old. She mastered clogging and continued to dance and compete until the age of seventeen. Suzan had prepared a videotape that chronicled Megan's life, and as Susan narrated the scenes, she smiled and expressed joy and pride in Megan. She related a story of an Irish Claddagh ring, that she gave to Megan and told her when she looked at it to remember she was always loved. The ring has a heart being held by two hands and a crown on top with Megan's birthstone. Later, this ring would help to positively identify Megan's body. Suzan now wears the ring in Megan's memory. When asked what would Megan's death rob her of, she stated that Megan was so looking forward to turning twenty-one. She had days marked on her calendar, counting down the time. (Megan was killed at age twenty and three months.) Suzan recalled how proud Megan was when she took her to her work place and showed off her first apartment. Megan liked being responsible.

The question was asked, how did you react to her disappearance? "I was confused and grasping to understand it. I kept asking to have it repeated." Suzan helped in the search for Megan, along with her brother A.J. But Suzan knew when they brought the chaplain to the search site that something was very wrong. What was the impact on her life? She had to have medication to sleep and still wakes up about the time of Megan's death each night. Still, she cannot enjoy a full moon because it reminds her of the night Megan died. They cremated Megan's body and Suzan has the ashes in her room. When asked why? She stated, "I am just not ready to let go of her yet." Her recounting this ordeal is so very painful to watch and listen to. When Quinn asked if there was anything that would help her to get closure, she replied that she did not know of anything. "Knowing the facts surrounding Megan's death would not help at all." Suzan stated that she had many thoughts of what Megan was going through as she laid in the canyon that night. "These thoughts are the most distressing thoughts for me, because I just feel in my heart that Megan died in that canyon." Suzan informed us that many of her friends at Camarillo State Hospital got together with her for Megan's twenty-first birthday, and erected a plaque, bench and planted a tree on the previous hospital grounds, which is now The University of California Channel Islands. I plan to go view it at the end of this trial.

Art, the father of Megan testified next. He was concerned that one of the last times he saw Megan, they had an argument. At the time, he asked Megan, "If you feel that way, why do you even come and see me?" Megan replied, "Because I love you, Dad." This touched Art so deeply, and at that point he said he "realized just what a beautiful, loving soul she was." He recalled their getting closer when she consulted him about wanting a relationship with a man. He told her, "Judge a man by his actions, not his words." Giving her fatherly advice was about life was a special moment for Art. When asked how he heard of the news of her disappearance, he recalled that the police came to his home after he had gotten off work that evening. He expressed that when he learned that a bullet hole had gone through her car and there was some blood found, "I knew she was in real trouble." He still expected Megan to call him, as she usually did when she was in trouble. He testified that after about two weeks of not recovering her body, he knew she was probably not alive. Art spend much time talking with the news people, because they were his only source of new information. He learned from them, that there were numerous bullet holes in the car. Once he learned that an AK-47 was the weapon used, it only compounded his horror. He had experience with this weapon while in Vietnam. He watched his buddies being shot, and remembers the sounds of it firing. He was very familiar with the damage that this weapon can do. Dobroth's voice cracked when she asked him how he felt when he knew that Megan, the same age that he was at the time of his Nam experience, was fired upon by an Ak-47 and had no protection or anyone to help her. Dobroth looked as if she would start to cry. Art sat stunned, and momentarily speechless. He recalled when he was fired upon in battle, he hit the ground and all he could think about was getting out of there. He stated he remembers wanting his mother. Art felt that Megan wanted him at that point in her life, and probably attempted to call him. "I imagine Megan was terrified, she was not in a war, she was not expecting to be shot at, she had no help. She probably wanted me to get her out of there." Witnessing the distress that a father feels when he cannot protect his little girl is just unbearable. My tears began to flow when he likened Megan to an orchid (he used to grow them). "She was just beginning her life and ready to blossom into a beautiful flower." Art refused to view the decomposed body of his daughter. He wanted to remember Megan as he had in life, full of spirit. But, he was present during one of the days of testimony where her body was shown in a photograph, and he looked up unwittingly. He told how he will never be able to get that picture out of his mind, and cannot believe that this is the same little girl that he used to read to. He states, "I now feels as if I am one-fifth dead. He had five children at the time of Megan's death and now part of him is gone." Art is not the happy, spontaneous person I knew five years ago at Camarillo State Hospital. I have not seen him smile or laugh one time during this process. He continues to remains very somber and contained.

Joyce (sexual assault victim) was the last witness for the first day of the Sentencing Hearing. She stated that in her culture, being Korean "meant that if something like this happens to you, you are damaged goods." Her extended family still does not know about her assault because of the shame it would bring on the family. Her father is in denial and her mother cannot bring herself to talk about it. Joyce urged her mother to go for therapy but after a couple of sessions, she dropped out because it was too hard to talk about. Joyce has gone to therapy for a year and a half now, but still exhibits a lot of distress. At first, she explained that she could not be alone, slept with the lights on and had to have her bedroom door shut at all times. Joyce expressed much anxiety, fear, and anger. She would lash out at her boyfriend but he remained very supportive of her. They later married. She stated that her boyfriend was strong through the whole experience and at one point, was her only support. Ironically, once she began to improve, he then began expressing a lot of anger. Telling her story seemed to be therapeutic for Joyce. Her voice seemed to get stronger. But she did get emotional when she related that Sanchez had given her a virus. When Quinn asked her how she knew, she started, "I had symptoms four days after the attack, went to the doctor and was diagnosed." Quinn asked would she be more reassured if she knew Sanchez had been tested for HIV? She stated, "No." He then cautiously probed, "we have been so personal already but could I ask what type of virus?" Joyce answered, "Herpes." "The reason she knows he gave it to her is because the symptoms arrived within days of their contact." Quinn then asked her, "is there anything else that you want to say at this time?" Joyce replied, "I just want people to know that just because a person looks okay on the outside, does not mean that they are really okay."

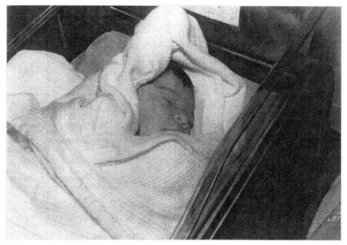

Megan Barroso, born March 15, 1981 to Suzan and Art Barroso

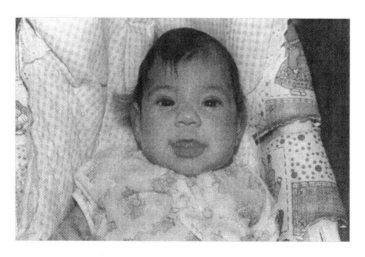

Megan was a healthy, happy baby.
Suzan called her "busy baby."

Megan and A.J. had the normal sibling rivalry at ages four and five.

Megan loved the beach

Megan made her mark on life early

Megan and A. J. ages three and four.

Megan loved dancing at an early age. This is her at nursery school.

Megan at the pumpkin patch

Suzan and Megan at
Saint Columbus Church,
San Diego Competition

Megan was very proud of
her clogging experiences.

Megan and Suzan at Squire Dance for
Conejo Valley Days Parade.

Megan at dance practice, age nine. She was described
as an advanced dancer early in her dance career.

Carol Ester (on right) was very instrumental in Megan's
continued involvement in clogging. Megan lived with
the Ester family and her life-long friend, Crickett while
she continued her education in Ventura County. This
also gave her the opporotunity to continue clogging.

Megan's Aunt Susie always loved this
photograph of Megan, age two and a half.

Megan as a young women. She is wearing The Claddagh ring
her mother gave her. The ring was a symbol that she was always
loved and also helped the rescue team to identify her body.

Megan and Crickett at the Ester home in Santa Rosa Valley, 1997. They have been friends since age seven.

Megan's friends attest to her easy smile and frequent laughter.

J.D. Berger

Investigator Richard Haas, Chief Prosecutor Leah Dobroth, And
Prosecutor Dee Corona attended the dedication ceremony to
honor Megan. They were extremely supportive of the Barroso
family and friends. City Council, Keith Milhouse looks on.

Suzan and A.J. at the Memorial for Megan, March 2002.

Clogging Memorial, Irish Step dancing They hold up
Megan's empty shoes to say good-bye. Her clogging
group still performs a dance in Megan's honor.

SENTENCING PHASE CONTINUES

Day two, we heard from Donna, Sanchez' last victim. This was the victim he assaulted five days after killing Megan. The same questions were asked of her as the other victims. How has this incident changed or impacted your life? Donna told how she and her family left their home the following day. She dyed her hair black and changed her appearance, because Sanchez had taken her driver's license and had her parents address. She had to get medication to sleep, and the first day she took ten pills with alcohol. She began drinking and later developed an alcohol abuse problem. She lost her job, and lost some of her friends, who thought it was her fault because she was attacked. This just blows my mind! I thought we were living in an age when people were more enlightened and informed. It amazes me that several of the assault victims' friends treated them this way. Donna was very angry and took out her rage on her current boyfriend. Her relationship with her mother became very strained, as Donna admitted to, "being mean for no reason." Donna, like the others, had a fear of being alone.

Her freedom was compromised because she could not go out at night. She stopped doing things with her friends. She has trouble sleeping, and even now re-lives the experience. Donna continues to have nightmares two years later. She went to an unconventional therapist who teaches Life Planning, and helped her get back what she wants her life to be. Donna stated she just woke up one morning and said, "I am tired of this. He took a year from my life but the next eighty will be on my terms." She changed her hair back to its' original color, began wearing her original clothing and sent out ten resumes. She got a job shortly thereafter. But to this day she feels guilt and asks herself, "Why Megan and not me?" (Survivor's guilt is a common phenomenon, which will cause victims to withdraw or sabotage their own success.) When asked if testifying gave her any closure, she stated, "the reason I came is so my mother didn't have to. I am doing it for Megan and her family." Donna exhibited much anger during her testimony and tried to make direct eye contact with Sanchez. He did not look up during her testimony, or during any others' this day.

Melissa, one of Megan's girlfriends tearfully spoke about how much Megan's friendship meant to her. They had been friends since High School and hung-out together daily. She said that Megan was always there for her and had been a great support when she lost her boyfriend in an auto accident. Megan's death impacted her life with sleep problems and job loss. Melissa too, has a fear of being alone. Sadly, Melissa learned of Megan's death while watching T.V.

Curstain's grandmother was visibly upset when she got on the stand. (Curstain was the baby girl whom Sanchez had battered and received a felony conviction at age twenty-two). Her response to testifying, "it dredges up old memories." Mrs.Conrad told how her son, Matthew, Dona (the baby's mother) and the baby had shared her home until

Dona moved out and then began living with Sanchez. Mrs. Conrad had never met Sanchez but he did call and threaten that he was coming for the baby. Mrs. Conrad changed their phone number the next day. Dona was sharing a place with Vincent Sanchez for three to four months before the 911 call went out that baby Curstain had stopped breathing. The next time the grandmother saw the baby; she had bruises on her head, patches of hair missing and had suffered weight loss. This was at Children's Hospital, where Curstain was in ICU for two days. Mrs. Conrad testified that after the mother and Sanchez were arrested for child abuse, the baby came back to live with the grandparents and her son, Matthew. Curstain was fearful and did not want to be around anyone but the grandparents. Curstain had stopped walking as a result of this ordeal but began to thrive again after several months in their care. She does not appear to have any permanent damage and is presently twelve years old.

Officer Donna Murren was the arresting officer that had responded to the 911 call regarding Curstain. She drove the mother and Sanchez to the hospital, as paramedics took the baby by ambulance. The story she got was that Sanchez was feeding the baby on the kitchen counter and she fell off, hitting her head. When he picked her up, she was not breathing so he took her into the bedroom where the baby's mother called 911. On the way to the hospital, the mother was crying and Sanchez was quiet. He made no attempt to comfort the mother. When they arrived Sanchez nonchalantly stated, "I need to take a piss." The officer said, "let's go in and see what is happening first." Dona and Vincent waited in the waiting area while Officer Murren went into the ER. The attending physician called attention to the baby as the staff backed up for the Officer to observe. Baby Curstain drew her arms to her body and clenched her fists in a fearful posture as they moved toward her. The physician indicated that this is a strong indicator of abuse.

Officer Murren went into the waiting room and advised Dona that she was under arrest for Child Endangerment. Sanchez had left the hospital. A warrant went out for his arrest and he was apprehended the following day and charged with Felony Corporal Injury to a Child. When asked how the Office could remember something that happened so long ago. She stated that she herself had an eleven-month old baby at that time.

A Los Angeles County Sheriff, Deputy Wilson told his version of the child endangerment story. He had interviewed Sanchez and Dona after their arrest. He had gotten a similar story from Sanchez as Officer Murren had but Sanchez added that he had given the baby the Heimlich to get her breathing again. Sanchez said that when he picked her up off the floor, she was not breathing, her eyes were rolled back, and she was listless. He explained to the Deputy that the bruises on her head were from giving her "noogies." When asked to explain, he stated that he would take his knuckle and hit her on the head when she was bad. Sanchez said that Curstain was, "Bad and her mother had spoiled her." He continued to say that they would put her in her crib for days as punishment when she was bad. He would not allow the mother to give her a bottle because, "She was too demanding of attention and cried a lot." Sanchez took control of feeding her. Dona was an eighteen-year-old mother and obviously not strong in asserting her rights as a mother. Obviously, neither had any concept of appropriate discipline for a baby.

This testimony is so extremely painful to listen to, but I can't help but think that it is healing for the victims and their families. Maybe my background makes me want to believe this is so. I felt sick to my stomach and a strong sense of anger toward Sanchez and the baby's mother, who did not protect her from his abuse.

The testimony of the abuse to this child was by far the most troubling testimony to date for me because she did not have any escape from the abuse and could not defend herself.

The day ended with Judge Riley allowing Prosecutor Dobroth to read a poem that Megan's friend, Kimberly wrote in her memory.

LAST WITNESSES
FOR PROSECUTION

The last two witnesses for the Prosecution were both physicians. Dr. Madihar was the admitting physician at Palmdale Emergency, the evening that Curstain Conrad came in by Paramedic escort. He was told that she was not breathing because she had fallen and choked on a carrot. Dr. Madihar described that their first procedure was to establish an airway. Once they could not locate any food in her throat, they "bagged her lungs." Bagging is when a mouthpiece in placed over the mouth and an airbag is pumped to force air into the lungs. Then the medical team put a tube into her lungs to open them up. The doctor explained how the tube entered the stomach first and had to be adjusted. This is very common with a very small child and does not cause any permanent damage if left only for a few minutes. Curstain was given an opiate blocker as a precaution that she might have swallowed some unknown medication. This is routine when the emergency staff is not clear why a child stops breathing. She was also given glucose to attempt to revive her. Dr. Madihar testified that Curstain was not responsive, only that she exhibited involuntary movements of her arms turning outward. This is a physiological response when breathing is a problem. He described her as "one step from comatose." The baby was given Valium so the medical team could place the tube into her lungs for respiratory therapy. The doctor explained that this is necessary because the human body will fight this procedure. She also continued to receive Valium throughout the procedures for a total of 12 milligrams. When asked if that was excessive, Dr. Deathers, the ICU Specialist for Children's Hospital later explained that as long as the tube is in the lungs, the patient must remain stationary. If the child moves her head, the tube can become dislodged and can damage the vocal cords. Dr. Madihar testified that he observed bruising on the side of Curstain's left head and face, and the crown of her head was soft. Also he could see that she was underweight for her age. He treated her from 7:00 p.m. until she was airlifted to Los Angeles Children's Hospital about 12:50 p.m. He felt that she needed more acute services than they had available at his small hospital in Palmdale. Also, this is protocol for treatment of children with this type of injury. Curstain was stable enough to transport at that time, as she was beginning to show some responsiveness. Dr. Madihar diagnosed Curstain with Malnutrition and Physical Abuse Trauma.

On March 25, 1992, Curstain arrived at Children's Hospital by helicopter. Dr. Deathers suspected that she had a seizure after hitting her head and this caused her to stop breathing. He said she was stable upon arrival at his hospital, but continued to be sedated. Children's repeated a CT Scan on the baby, and got better results. (Palmdale was unable to get a readable CT Scan.) The test revealed bleeding on the brain, and retinal hemorrhaging. This is when the back of the eyes bleed and can damage the device that allows us vision. He stated this could only be done by a severe blow to the head or shaking. He went on to say that one shake or a minor fall will not cause this type of injury. There were signs that Curstain had previous injury to her brain, which was evident by spaces in the cavity. New injuries (red areas on the CT Scan) are compounded and become more severe because of the older injuries. He stated that the original injuries were at least one month old. He diagnosed Curstain with Battered Child Syndrome. The malnutrition, bruising, and brain trauma are consistent with this diagnosis. Her bruises indicated old and new ones, because they ranged in color from red, purple, black, yellow and green. He also noted that she had hair missing on the back of her head. "It looked as though it had been pulled out." When asked if these injuries could have been fatal, he stated that if she had not received quick medical attention at Palmdale hospital, she could have suffered permanent brain damage or death. Dr. Deathers treated Curstain for two days in Intensive Care. By 8:00 a.m. the following morning, Curstain was expressing words, feeding and giving eye contact. She was transferred onto the medical floor on March 27, 1992, where she remained until her discharge on April 5, 1992.

This is some of the most depressing testimony to date for many of us. The air was so thick in the jury room; you could cut it with a knife. It just breaks my heart to hear that anyone could do injury to a child. I wondered what Sanchez could have been thinking as he sat through this testimony. At this point in time, all I felt for him was animosity! Would I be able to muster any compassion for him? Time will tell.

SANCHEZ' FATHER SPEAKS

Mariano Sanchez, Vincent's dad, spent hours on the stand. He presented himself as a very proud man. He considered himself the father of all of Margaret's children, even though she had five children when they married. They have been married for thirty-seven years now and have a total of eight children. Mariano was a hardworking man and spent much time out of town and long hours on his job. He did construction work; mostly concrete fittings for freeway pillows and buildings. Margaret, Vincent's mother had most of the responsibility for the children's care. She was a religious woman and her husband was a heavy drinker. He testified that at the time, he did not consider himself an alcoholic because everyone in the industry drank. Mariano would carry a 12-pak of beer in his lunch pail to work. Although he stated he was too busy to drink on the job. He does not feel that his drinking ever contributed to any injuries while at work.

Mariano has been described as an abusive man, "a mean drunk." He disputes this. When asked if he hit his wife, he replied, "I may have, once or twice." But he was adamant about not hitting his kids or being abusive to them. He stated one time; he hit his son, Anthony in the stomach with his fist because Anthony had taken his car without permission. He also admitted that he and his wife argued and yelled at each other, but denied ever injuring her. They had separated at one time for six or seven months and Margaret had planned to divorce him. But they eventually got back together. Mariano started that Vincent was, "his baby boy." Vincent was known as Mariano's clone and would insist on being wherever Mariano was. Vincent would spend the weekends with him while he and Margaret were separated. Even though Mariano told his wife he would never have his boys do the type of work that he did, he finally took Vincent to his job and hired him.

Vincent was eager to please. His father described him as a hard worker and he also pushed other workers to complete tasks. Vincent was hit with a boom and received some permanent injury to his shoulder and one leg. This was the start of Vincent going through inconsistent periods of employment. Mariano was requested to testify at the insurance disposition. In his mind it was more like "an inquisition."

Mariano told the court that he loved his son, Vincent and all of his kids. He said, "Vincent did good in school because if he did not, I would have heard." But he never saw any of Vincent's wrestling matches, claiming he was at work. Mariano claimed that the family was very close, yet there were many things about Vincent that he did not know. For instance, he did not know when Vincent quit High School, or the details of his motorcycle accident in tenth grade. Mariano accompanied Vincent to court in 1992, but did not know the nature of the proceedings. When Vincent went to Prison, his dad did not know. He was aware that Vincent was incarcerated but thought maybe he was in jail. When asked why he did not ask Vincent about it, he stated, "Vince was a man, that was his business." Mariano denied knowing about Vincent's anger problems, his drinking problem, or any of his criminal behaviors. He was not aware of his artistic abilities until recently, when one of the investigators showed him Vincent's drawings. When asked about the charges against Vincent, his dad knew none of the details and stated coldly, "that is not the Vincent I knew."

What Mariano did know about Vincent was that he was hardworking, very helpful to others without their asking, kind, respectful of women, and competitive. When asked if the competitiveness of Vincent created a problem, he stated proudly, "He always wanted to out-do the old man." The father described the family as active. They went boating, camping, fishing and target shooting together.

The Prosecution asked Mariano about his parenting skills. Did he instill morals, and family values in his kids? He stated he "tried to, especially with the girls." Why the girls? Were they treated differently from the boys? He replied, "I did not want them to leave the nest." When asked if he abused any of them or their mother, he stated "no." When asked about how he disciplined the children, he stated that he was "firm." Prosecutor Corona asked Mariano if any sexual aggression was condoned in the Sanchez household. He replied in an indignant fashion, "not at all."

Mariano stopped drinking in 1989, following a near death experience. He was seriously injured and spent thirty-seven days in the hospital. He said he expired once while there. The father then began to go to church with his wife, and became a born-again Christian. After quitting drinking and smoking, he would not allow anyone in his house to drink or smoke. He admitted previously to blackouts or passing out due to heavy drinking. Also, at times he did not remember everything about his behavior while being intoxicated. Mariano stated that he never hit his wife or abused her in front of his kids. But his children will tell a different story.

Kathie (the oldest) and Marion (the youngest) sisters of Vincent told similar stories about their home-life. Their dad was an abusive drunk. He hit their mom as well as the children. On one occasion, he knocked Margaret unconscious. Another time, he broke one of her fingers. The parents yelled and argued a lot in front of the children. The girls testified that the children would leave the room or go hide when Mariano had been drinking heavy. They verified the "rainy day syndrome" that the Defense had introduced earlier. When their dad was home on rainy days, he drank and usually to the point of getting intoxicated. The children would dread coming home after school on these days. Marion stated that they stayed quiet, went to their rooms or watched T.V. to avoid his wrath. Marion said that her dad never hit her because she was, "his baby girl." Also, Vincent was favored because he was the youngest boy. She also told how the children would get scared and go to their rooms when they heard their dad's truck turn onto their street if it was after dark. This meant he had already been drinking for a while and would be ill tempered. The Defense wanted to talk about other types of abuse in the household but Kathie had already stated she did not want to talk about this. The jury was sent out while the attorneys spoke with the judge. The subject was changed upon our return, leaving us wondering what was not told.

The girls also recalled some good times in the Sanchez family household. They went boating, camping, and to

Disneyland as a family. They loved their dad and since he quit drinking, had seen a complete change in him.

A neighbor who had been close to the Sanchez family, Julius Cooper was called to the stand next. He told of playing basketball almost everyday after work with Vincent and the kids in the neighborhood. He said that his house was the hangout spot for all the kids because they had a basketball net. He felt close to Vincent and continued to visit him even after he had left the family home. Julius testified that he was not aware of any abuse going on in the Sanchez household. He expressed affection for Mrs. Sanchez by stating, "Mom was real quiet, not very independent, like a submissive but a religious woman." Julius said that he always felt accepted by the Sanchez family and felt that they would do anything to help him.

Rose, a neighbor of Vincent's while on Woodrow Street, testified that Vincent had always been very polite and protective of her. She had been a girlfriend of Steve Preu, one of Vincent's roommates. Rose has Muscular Sclerosis and has a very difficult time walking. She stated that Vincent would help her back down the street when she was tired and ready to go home. When asked how she would describe Vincent, she laughed and stated, "He's a dork." Rose had never witnessed Vincent being rude to any females.

DEFENSE EXPERT
INTRODUCED

The Defense called Art Soto, a neighbor who knew Vincent's when he was fifteen years old. Mr. Soto described he and Vincent as "best friends." They worked on cars together, and Vincent helped him with his yard. Art said Vincent was always at his house, but never knew of any problems in his family life. He verified the motorcycle accident that Vincent had in tenth grade. A friend give them rides to school on his motorcycle, and one day they were hit. Vincent ended up with a broken leg. Art testified that gradually Vincent stopped going to school after that. He was aware that Vincent had a great interest in wrestling but was not sure if his inability to wrestle was the reason he quit school.

Mr. Soto told the court that Vincent lived with him for seven to eight months at one time. Vincent paid rent and helped him financially. When asked how he felt when he heard what Vincent had been charged with, he replied he was shocked. Many of Vincent's friends and neighbors saw a completely different side of his personality.

Doctor Amy Phenix, a Clinical Psychologist working at California Men's Colony gave the most believable interpretation of Vincent's mental functions. Her experience was with Mentally Disturbed Offenders and Sexually Violent Predators at Atasadero State Hospital. She was asked by the Defense to evaluate Sanchez for his mental disturbance. Dr. Phenix diagnosed Sanchez as Borderline Personality Disorder/Anti-social and Paraphilia. She described Paraphilia as consisting of one or all of three things: Sexually aggressive toward a non-consenting partner, Voyeurism and Fetish behavior. She explained that Sanchez has all three of these conditions. "He wants to have sex with a female who does not give consent, to control her. He collects photos, and tapes them through their windows to view later to feed his sexual fantasy. And he has a fetish of taking their panties and personal items as souvenirs." Dr. Phenix feels that Sanchez has abandonment issues. She describes him as very needy, almost in a panic state when his needs are not met. This is why he attached himself to Luz and became so compulsive in pursuing the relationship. The less he could control her, the more he tried and the more obsessed he became. When she pushed him away, he would panic and exert more control and cling to her. This was evidenced by the sixty-five phone calls in a few days time, and is characteristic of Borderline Personality Disorder. I have worked with some persons with this type of disorder. We describe it as, "I hate you, don't leave me" syndrome. Sanchez told Dr. Phenix, "Luz was the air he breathes." He told Dr. Phenix that Luz made him feel more loved than anyone had ever made him feel. He truly believed he could not live without her. So when she broke up with him, he freaked out and wanted to kill himself, her or both. This was explained as the, " affection to rage continuum." She continued to explain that we see this many times when a person will kill their loved ones and then theirself. Dr. Phenix felt that it was just a matter of time before Sanchez would have committed a crime like murder. When asked if she felt he knew right from wrong, she adamantly stated, "yes." He knew he was out of control and stated in their interview, "He wanted to be caught. He was tired." Dr. Phenix explained that Sanchez' extreme emotional disturbance made him homicidal/suicidal. This explanation also sheds some light on his reaction to the Conrad baby. He was jealous of Curstain and the attention she took away from him, to the point of almost killing her. Obviously, he had a very dysfunctional relationship with the baby's mother as well.

"Sanchez has cognitive distortions," Dr. Phenix continued. These were explained as extremely misguided concepts of himself and how women perceived him. He knew it was wrong to force himself on women but he thought that once the sex act started, they would like him. This is how the "dating behavior" was explained in his assaults. When asked about how Tonya must have felt once he viewed the video of her rape, Sanchez stated, "she did not look like she liked it, but at the time I was not aware of her feelings." "This ability to detach from the victims' feelings is what makes the assaults possible, explained Dr. Phenix. By thinking that these women like him, he can justify his actions and go on to re-offend. He can control his urges to rape by some extent. But when he drank, he had less control over all of his emotions." His pattern of assaults were about every four to six months and in the interim, he would satisfy himself by watching the videos of his sexual encounters. Sanchez' behavior was described as a compulsion that he showed little control over. Dr. Phenix affirmed that she had read Dr. Prentky's report and verified that he was a well-known researcher in the area of sexual abuse. I was please when Dr. Phenix stated that she did agree with the verdicts of the jury in this case. I don't think Quinn was happy once he had asked the question. He looked a bit taken-aback by her response.

Five and one-half hours Dr. Phenix spent interviewing Sanchez. Vincent told the doctor that at one point he became so disgusted with his behavior that he destroyed many of the videos and photos he had taken, in an effort to stop assaulting. Maybe he was aware enough to know that this was helping to feed his dysfunction. Dr. Phenix feels that Sanchez does make choices about his behavior, just as we all do. But she also feels that his choices are altered by his thinking errors. Dr. Phenix also feels that he does have some control over his compulsive sexual drive, as evidenced by the fact that he did not offend more often. "But when he is in a heightened stress state, feeling needy or abandoned, he will go into a panic mode. This is when he needs to exert control over Luz. If not her, another female like her. He acts out the rage that has been building inside him." When asked why or when this rage came about, she stated that she thought it started in his childhood and has grown from there. The Prosecution objected to this comment, saying this was only speculation on her part.

Many other things were brought to the forefront about Sanchez' behavior today. He set a fire when he was ten (accidentally, he said), stole marijuana from a neighbor and took it to school to show off, and stole a car stereo from someone living near him. I had suspected that he must have had some earlier criminal behavior. Also, it was mentioned that he attempted to fraud the insurance company on his injury case by malingering. When the doctor was asked if she knew some of his threats to harm himself were untrue, or used to manipulate Luz, Dr. Phenix agreed that persons with this disorder do tend to manipulate others. She did not think Sanchez' efforts were very successful because the manipulation often did not work for him. Prosecutor Corona stated Vincent once told a girlfriend that he had a brain tumor when she attempted to break up with him. Evidence points to the fact that he never had healthy relationships with females he dated.

Finally, someone gave Sanchez a forensic evaluation! But the problem is, nobody pursued what it reflected. The questions continued on the mental illness explanation. Dr. Phenix saw no evidence that Sanchez had a head injury, nor had she been told anything about one. When asked if this would have been helpful to know, she stated, "Definitely." (This appears to be an important fact for her evaluation.) Here seems to be another case when the Defense just tells the facts that they want to tell, to get the results they want. Another important fact that came out today was that Sanchez never really took advantage of any treatment that was offered him. He left the hospital before they ever knew his real problem, stopped taking the free medications, stopped making his appointments for free treatment, and began drinking again. Dr. Phenix stated that this is quite common with people needing treatment. They don't have the insight to realize that they can't handle their own problems. I suspect it was more that Sanchez only asked for help when he thought it would win over Luz. Once he realized this did not work, he went back to his old behaviors. He admitted to starting to increase his drinking a couple of months following his discharge from the hospital. He lead his brother, Anthony to believe that the Mental Health facility had nothing to offer him. When in reality, he was referred for Anger Management and Substance Abuse treatment, but did not pursue either.

FAMILY AND FRIENDS TESTIFY

The following witnesses for the Defense were various family members and neighborhood friends. Frank, Vincent's brother became weepy almost as soon as he got on the stand. He related much of the some story that others have given. His father drank too much, got mean when he drank and abused the children, as well as their mother. When asked anything about the abuse or discipline of the children, Frank would start to wring his hands or use tissue to wipe them excessively. I fear that there are many secrets in this family. And I believe much shame and guilt. Nobody seems to want to really tell the story completely. At first, I thought it was because they feared that Mariano could be prosecuted for some of his past behaviors. It seems that Frank might have gotten a greater share if the abuse by the way his is reacting in court.

When Frank spoke about his love for his brother Vincent, his demeanor changed. He stated that Vincent had many good characteristics to his personality. He was particularly pleased with the relationship that Vincent had with his boys. He stated that he had a sixteen year old that was going through some rough times right now, and Vincent had given him encouragement to stay in school and continue with sports. Frank broke down and sobbed when asked how he felt about Vincent having to live the rest of his life in prison. He stated, "I love him. This little guy means the world to me."

Carmen Sanchez, considered herself a friend to Vincent. Her daughter, (whose name is also Carmen) had a baby girl by Vincent's brother, Mariano. Mrs. Sanchez described her relationship with Vincent as one of mutual respect and helpfulness. She felt he would do anything for her and her family. Vincent would drop by often and acted as a handyman for her. Carmen felt that Vincent acted more like a father to Mariano's baby girl than he did. Vincent would watch the baby when Carmen was busy with dinner and even buy her diapers on some occasions. Carmen testified that Vincent had enriched her life in many ways.

Shannon Stout had been a neighbor of the Sanchez family during the 1990's. Vincent came around a lot and was like a family member. He was a friend to her mother as well, and would sit and visit with her when Shannon was not home. Shannon felt that Vincent wanted a more serious relationship with her, but did not think her family wanted it. When questioned why, she stated, "He drank too much and was older than me." However, she continued to say that Vincent never drank in their house or showed any disrespect for her or her family. She and Vincent would have spats during their friendship but this did not stop him from visiting with her mother, Jeanette. After Vincent began dating Luz, Shannon did not see much of him. But Shannon also was dating at the time.

Jeanette Moak, the mother of Shannon told the court how she loved Vincent as a son. Their relationship continued for a number of years. Jeanette seemed to know Vincent better than most of his friends did. When he was depressed or something was bothering him, she recognized it. Even then, they did not talk in real detail about things, as one would expect close friends to do. Maybe their age difference was the reason. One of the things that strike me as odd is that nobody seems to really breech any sensitive subjects with Vincent. Jeanette stated she knew when Shannon and Vincent were having a riff but did not know much else about things troubling him. However, she did recognize that he had some depression following his crane accident. Because of this, she would try to get him out of his house as much as possible.

A landscaper, Jeff Sullivan hired Vincent at age seventeen, to help him with his business. He viewed Vincent as a hard worker, helpful and dependable. They also had been neighbors and have remained friends to the present. When Jeff moved his family to Utah, Vincent helped. This appears to be a recurring theme. (Other witnesses have told how Vincent helped them move.) Jeff says that even in the recent past, Vincent has popped in to visit his family. He did not mind this because he enjoyed seeing him. Finally, when asked if he knew what Vincent had been doing to young women back then, Jeff stated, "No, but I trusted him with my three girls."

To our surprise, Margaret, Vincent's mother took the stand. After hearing others testify about her, I thought that she would be this weak, timid lady. She actually did well. She spoke in a soft voice but answered many of the difficult questions about her husbands drinking and abuse toward the family. Margaret downplayed the abuse allegations, stating, "In this day and age, everything is abuse." She did admit that Mariano was rough with his punishment. One incident she recalled was when the police had caught Vincent with a stolen car stereo. Margaret related that Mariano took off his belt and began whipping Vincent in front of the policemen. When asked what the police did, she replied, "They walked away." Margaret, like the other family members was guarded about what she told to the court. She began to cry when she related that this was all very painful for the family. "Mariano is very embarrassed and ashamed by what is being said about him." For this reason, she was inclined to not say much, "Because the newspapers will print it."

Margaret gave a completely different story about Mariano once he received the Lord. She was so proud of the changes that he had made and likened him to a different person. She had tried for many years to get him to go to church with her. Then one day, he put on a suit and went. Defense Attorney Helfrich became very tender when she asked the rhetorical question, "And he did it very proud, didn't he?" Ms. Helfrich took a second to regain her composer before asking the next question. This is a reminder to us of how involved attorneys get in their work and the lives of their clients.

Ted Sebodoa returned to court to speak about Vincent's character. He spoke about all the times Vincent had been there for him. Many times when nobody asked for his help. His son had grown up with Vincent and wanted him as best man at his wedding. It was apparent that Ted was attached to Vincent in a fatherly way. They spent many hours working on some of Ted's old collectible cars. Recently, Vincent had presented him with a drawing of one of his favorite cars, as well as a fire truck like his son T.J. drove. Ted shared these drawings with the court like a proud father. His voice cracked when he stated, "I love Vincent and want him to be around in the future."

Another employer testified to Vincent's good work habits. He had hired him to help paint multi-million dollar homes. He told how trustworthy Vincent was, and that customers often praised him for his politeness. Then he related an incident when Vincent had helped him to recover some equipment that had been stolen by another employee. Even after he was told that Vincent had served some time in prison, he re-hired him. But he expressed complete shock when he was told about his sexual crimes.

Vincent's sister, Francine informed the court that her family was extremely upset that she was testifying in court. She felt that her testimony would help Vincent and the rest of the family to heal. Francine acknowledged that the family had been hiding this big secret for years. She remembers her home life as "chaotic." Her story resounded what other members had said. Mariano did not act the same in public as he did in the home. However, she was sure that the neighbors knew about his drinking and abuse because he was so loud. If Mariano got angry, he would make the children go to their rooms for the rest of the day, even if it was still daylight outside. When questioned if she exaggerated about his behavior she answered, "These are the things that stuck in my mind." She seems to be the most forthright in her testimony of all the family, thus far. Which might explain why there was some family resistant to her getting on the stand. Francine remembers Vincent getting punished a lot. She also remembered that Mariano's "real" children were the favored ones. He would buy them things. Francine remembers Vincent getting punished by his dad and then being told he was going with him when he left the house. This was a bit troubling to me. What kind of treatment did he get once away from the home? Especially, since he was angry with him already. Several of the Sanchez children have alluded to horrible things but the facts seem to get hushed before completely brought out. So, we jurors are left to ponder what it might be. I began to suspect some sexual abuse may have occurred in their household. Francine verified that the children would become fearful when their dad came home late, and would scatter and hide. She explained his behavior as "predictable." If he came home late then he would be drunk. And if he were drunk, he would be mean and yell at everyone. Francine remembers the boys getting more punishment than the girls, however. She managed to stay out of his wrath most of the time but did get pushed around the times she attempted to call the police on him. Francine still did not tell us of any deep dark secrets. She also acknowledges that they did do fun things as a family.

Francine's husband, Peter verified her stories about living in the Sanchez household. He had been going there since he started dating her in his early twenties. Peter had witnessed Mariano being abusive to his sons on several occasions. One time he related, when Vincent was about fifteen, he had upset his dad and so he was told to sit against a wall in the garage. When Peter returned to their home five or six hours later, Vincent was still sitting in the same spot. Francine had also told of time-out sessions for Vincent that was excessive. Like father, like son. Mariano had sure taught Vincent some poor childrearing skills! It is amazing that the children in this family turned out to be as productive as they are. Peter shared another story of Mariano becoming upset with Frank and Andrew, and preceded to chase them across the street. As they ran behind a car, Mariano grabbed Peter and began choking him. Once he discovered that he had grabbed the wrong boy, he laughed and held him while he gave him a noogie on his head. Mariano stated, "You are not my boy. I'd better not hit you. You might knock the crap out of me." Peter was hoping that his testifying would help Francine to recover. He was aware of how upsetting and stressful this was for her. He also wanted their children to have respect for their parents and to feel loved. Peter echoed the same story told by Francine, "Mariano showed favoritism to the younger kids by giving Mariano Jr. a Mustang, Vincent a truck, and Marian a house."

Vincent's sister-in-law, Pamela testified on his behalf. Now divorced, she had been married to his brother, Frank for eight years. She still maintained a friendship with Vincent. Pamela had been instrumental in introducing Luz to Vincent at a church camp-out. Pamela also testified that Vincent would get out of hand when he drank too much. But she would never have suspected that he had any problems such as the ones that have been recently exposed. She told the court that she plans to continue her relationship with him, "Because I feel there is still a good person inside." Pamela testified that she had never witnessed any improper behavior on Vincent's part toward any females. Also, she will continue to encourage the friendship that he shares with her daughter, even though the girl's father does not.

Obviously, none of the family or friends who testified on Vincent's behalf condoned his behavior. All expressed shock and surprise because they felt they knew a totally different person than the one being described here in court. They were all present to express their desire to see Vincent live, and felt he could continue to add to their lives. Most all stated they would continue to support him and keep in contact with him.

Annette Town, the Defense Investigator was called to the stand to submit into evidence some drawings that Vincent had given her and various Defense team members around Christmas time, 2002. This worked to draw on our sentiment and showed us another side to Vincent. His drawing abilities were not known before his incarceration.

MORE EXPERTS

By the end of the second week of the Sentencing Phase, the Defense had called twenty-one witnesses. Dave Berlin owned an air conditioning business and had employed Vincent because he was a hard worker, and would do the jobs that others refused to do. Such jobs as going into the attic, under extremely hot conditions. He testified that Vincent was polite and always on time to work. Then later told us that he picked him up for work and took him home each day. Dave knew nothing of Vincent's past behaviors, even though they did have "guy talk" while on the job.

Dr. Mary Jane Adams was an impressive witness. She had worked in the field of Criminology and with Sexual Offenders for many years, nine of them while at Patton State Hospital. Her experience also included treatment with survival victims of violent sexual assaults. She continued this work after she went into private practice. For this consultation, she was being paid $150.00 per hour. She testified thus far she had put in approximately 40-50 hours of work on this case, not including her testimony time. Dr. Adams spent nine hours just interviewing Sanchez. This appeared to be the most time anyone had thus far. The time seems to have paid off, as she obtained information that others had not gotten from him.

Vincent Sanchez told Dr. Adams he had been sexually molested at age ten by a cousin. Dr. Adams suspected that he had been raped while in Prison in his early twenties also. Sanchez did not volunteer this information, but Dr. Adams knew enough about the Prison environment to know that many times a small man will be the victim of such crimes. This rings true to me also, because he already had broken the code of criminals by hurting a child. Even hardened criminals view this behavior as the worse thing you can do and would show no mercy. I also doubt that he got much protection from the prison guards. Which might lend some insight into why Sanchez had such rage toward male authority figures, such as policemen. Dr. Adams feels that his anger was not toward females, as odd as that may seem. She confirmed that he only used as much force as needed to control his victims. "He was not a sadistic rapist and his goal was not to severely harm them," she asserted.

Sanchez had experienced a heightened sexual relationship with his girlfriend, Dona around the age of twenty. He worried that he was not sure that he could please her sexually. Apparently, this is when the fetish with thong panties began. Another event that played a part in his violent sexual behavior was seeing a man looking into someone's room at a hotel, and masturbating. Sanchez admitted to repeating that behavior after the man left. This is the point when Dr. Adams feels the voyeurism began. Sanchez also told her of a time when he was looking into windows and witnessed a man pushing a woman onto a bed in a very rough manner. The doctor felt that these incidents left imprints on his brain. She discussed in length about the wiring of the brain and how experiences repeated over time, can impact the critical thinking processes. Examples were people who witnessed much violence at an early age. It has a connection to the fight or flight response in all of us, conditioning a person for anxiety and fear. A child feels they must develop coping strategies to deal with the fact that nobody will protect them. They come up with their own ways of getting their needs met. Many times they began using manipulation of others for their own purposes. Dr. Adams confirmed that Sanchez had a Paraphilic Disorder and described the same three areas that Dr. Phenix had: sex with non-consenting persons, voyeurism, and fetish behaviors. She also agreed with the Borderline Personality Diagnosis. Dr. Adams has worked with many Sexual Offenders over the years, and has seen a pattern. Most all persons with this disorder had two things in common: molestation at an early age, and a personality disorder. The doctor described how this type of person would split their thinking. Splitting is defined as, having a child-like thinking pattern. When a person is viewed as all good or all bad, and the child cannot entertain, as most adults can, that we all have some good and bad characteristics. "This is why we sometimes see the Jetkyl and Hyde personality type. They hate you or love you." Sanchez described his mom as "a saint." And what he told the doctor about his father was that, "He loved him very much and always tried to please him." Dr. Adams did not think that Sanchez liked his father very much. He related to her an incident when he witnessed his father beating up his sisters' boyfriend.

When asked by the Prosecution about Sanchez having free-will, Dr. Adams responded, "Free-will is defined by what choices we make through understanding." She did not, and still does not believe that Sanchez has a true understanding why he did the things he did. She expressed that she did not want to go too deeply into his painful past because she was concerned about him going back into his cell with no help in dealing with the feelings that would certainly be brought to the surface. Dr. Adams stated that two things are always present as a motivator for Borderline Personality Types: trust and power. They don't trust others to meet their needs or truly care for them, and they need to feel a sense of power over their environment. Sanchez admitted that he was pleased that, "He could out-smart the cops in Simi." He laughed when he related that, "Simi was supposed to be a safe little community." Sanchez seemed to feel pleased that he could cause everyone to be fearful.

Another factor that is usually present in this diagnosis is poor self-esteem and self-worth. Sanchez sure was a good example of that. He always wanted to have an attractive girlfriend. One of the reasons he had a love for wrestling was, "he could get attention from the girls." Apparently, this reassured him about his own manliness. He had some real identity problems and doing well at the sport of wrestling gave him a sense of who he was. However, his family never supported this ability in him by attending any of his matches.

When asked by the Prosecution why Sanchez did not take advantage of all the mental health services that were offered him, Dr. Adams expressed that this is very typical. Most persons of this type either don't have the insight to know that they really need the help, or think they can manage it by themselves. In Sanchez' case, he was also afraid of being found out. "If he stayed in treatment, eventually he would be forced to confront his painful past in order to work through it. Many of us who don't have major personality problems will avoid working on things that bring us pain once remembered."

Finally, Dr. Adams discussed some current studies being done with sex offenders. Hazelton published a study stating that sexual offenders will most always commit a crime of murder during the course of their offenses. That is a staggering thought! Hazelton has the reputation of reliable research in this field for many years. Another study being conducted by Kaiser on the early brain wiring theory, involves 18,000 subjects. These subjects are taken from the public who have come to Kaiser for other services and agreed to complete their survey. The survey consists of questions addressing: a history of having been sexually, emotionally, or physically abused, observed parental violence in the home where law officials had to intervene, being witness to parental fighting or abuse, or being a victim of domestic violence. It will be very interesting to hear the results of this study.

THE MUCH AWAITED
DR. DIETZ

I had a horrible dream last night. I dreamt I came upon an accident and saw bodies spread all over the ground. There were so many pieces of mangled auto parts and body parts that I could hardly make sense of it. To my dismay, I wondered how could this happen? What can I do? This case is much like my dream. Coming upon a scene after the fact and trying to make sense of it all. There seems to be so many pieces to this puzzle. Will we ever know the truth?

We seem to get a bit closer to truth with each day and every witness. Today we heard from a very renowned expert witness, Dr. Park Dietz. He is a Harvard graduate in the field of Psychiatry. Much of his experience has been with John Hopkins University. He also has extensive experience with Mental Disabilities. He also worked for the FBI as a profiler. Currently, he has a firm with fifty associates who are expert in their various fields. Four of his team worked on this case as consultants for the Prosecution. To date, they have put in countless hours and without factoring in his testimony, the bill is at $90,000. Dr. Dietz receives $600 an hour for his services. Some of the high profile cases he has worked on are: John Hinckley, who tried to kill President Reagan. Jeffrey Dahmer, who killed and ate young men. The Unabomber, who evaded the police for many years. The Menendez Brothers, who murdered their parents, claiming they had been sexually abused. The Columbine School shootings, where two young boys opened fire on their classmates. Andrea Yates, the mother who drown all her children. And the stalking murder of Rebecca Schaffer, a T.V. actress. Since he was testifying for the Prosecution and had very impressive credentials, the Defense confronted him immediately. Quinn inquired, "We know you don't have a reputation for being a hired gun, but don't you take cases where you believe the defendant is guilty?" Dr. Dietz responded by saying, "I take cases with the attempt to use my skills to get to the truth, whether it be for the Defense or the Prosecution. It would serve nobody' purpose if the truth is not obtained." Quinn made several argumentative statements to him before finally apologizing for his behavior.

Quinn's goal was to attempt to poke holes in Dr. Dietz theories. He questioned his diagnosis of Sanchez for Anti-Social Personality Disorder. Dr. Dietz stated that Sanchez did have enough of the factors before the age of fifteen years old that would make it a possible diagnosis. They were as follows: Breaking the law; setting a fire, stealing a car stereo, being truant from school, showing impulse control problems, lying and deceition, robbery, and substance abuse. If detected before age fifteen, many times this diagnosis is considered Conduct Disorder. Dr. Dietz states that a person only needs three areas to be identified as Conduct Disorder, which Sanchez had, along with evidence of seven factors for Anti-Social Disorder. Dietz sited examples of Sanchez using lies and deception to represent himself to many of the people who knew him. That is why so many people could not believe that he had done such heinous crimes. To his friends and neighbors, he showed a charming and helpful side. Sanchez also tried twice to defraud the Workmen's Compensation Program. Once telling them he could barely move but then was caught jet skiing at the lake. Another misrepresentation was telling personnel at county jail that he was hallucinating. This was probably an attempt to get drugs. He also manipulated the system by attending alcohol classes with the knowledge he would get time off his jail sentence.

Dr. Phenix had diagnosed Sanchez as Borderline Personality Disorder, NOS (not otherwise specified), Anti-social and Paraphilia. Dr. Adams had diagnosed him with Borderline Personality Disorder and Paraphilia. Dr. Dietz feels that Sanchez has a Personality Disorder but that Anti-social is more correct. He agrees with the Paraphilic disorder and explains there are two parts to it: A). The desire and B). The action one takes with disregard for harm to others. The doctor describes that not all Paraphilic will go on to commit a crime. Some find acceptable ways to relieve their desires, such as looking at a magazine and masturbating, or visiting a prostitute. He disagrees with the medical profession in the Diagnostic and Statistics Manual regarding the assertion that a crime must be committed to be a Paraphilic. He feels that a person can still be a Paraphilic without acting on it in a criminal manner. "Many persons come to our attention because they do commit crimes, however." Quinn tried everything he could to discredit Dietz on his views. Quinn probes, "So if they agree with you, then they are correct?" Dr. Dietz has had much experience with testifying and did not react to Quinn's comments. He stated, "When it comes to principles, then they take priority over theory." Meaning he chose to hold to his views regardless of who agreed or disagreed with him. He quoted his twenty-five years in the field as his reason. He also verified that thirty-five to fifty percent of criminals in prison were sexually molested. And if you take away the drug-related crimes, the number goes up to about seventy percent. This is a staggering statistic! Sanchez refused to discuss the sexual abuse with Dietz. But Dietz had reviewed the notes of Dr. Phenix and Dr. Adams, to whom Sanchez had disclosed his experiences. Sanchez told Adams he had been raped at age ten, and also three times while incarcerated in prison. According to Sanchez, he began his sexual assaulting two months after leaving prison.

Sanchez related his method of operation to Dr. Dietz regarding his sexual offenses. He began with surveillance of a neighborhood. He would see a pretty female and follow her into the neighborhood. Then he would drive the area day and night to learn the routine of people living there. Peeping into the windows and homes would be next. He would also listen for names, so he could use them later when conversing with his victims. Photographing and videotaping would be used with some, not all. If someone came upon him while in the area, he would pretend that he was gardening or checking the water sprinklers. Next, he would go into the victims home and listen. He found out who was there and where they slept. Looking for escape routes and where the phones were located became an important step. At the time he was in the home, he might take articles of clothing, like thong panties. (My mind flashed to the thought that this might have been how Megan ended up with her own thong panties on that night. I continue to be troubled by how she was found in them, when she did not go home to change and Kimberly had seen her in cotton panties earlier.) Finally, Sanchez would go back for the sexual assault.

Sanchez admitted to Dr. Dietz of peeping on at least fifty females and photographing at least thirty, for later viewing. Sanchez also told the doctor that he was very proud of himself, for the good job he did at, "out-smarting the police."

Dr. Dietz said that if he had to give his disorder a one-word description, it would be, "fearless."

Quinn tried to get Dr. Dietz to consider a diagnosis of Post Traumatic Stress Disorder. Although Sanchez had been raped and had two factors; irritability and aggression, he did not fit the category according to Dietz. Quinn's attempts to get Dr. Dietz to say Sanchez has an Impulse Disorder did not fly either. Dr. Dietz also expounded that Paraphilia does not imply an impulse disorder. He upset Quinn by saying that the diagnosis of Intermittent Explosive Disorder is a joke! And any one in their profession knows this, unless they are naïve." They argued about what the Diagnostic Manual maintains for some time but Dr. Dietz prevailed. After all, he had helped to write the manual!

Quinn thought he had Dietz when he quoted a portion of a 60 Minutes Interview that featured Dr. Dietz on profiling. Dr. Dietz told the interviewer that he would play a game with his young son while at Disneyland, called "Spot the Psychopath." Everybody was roaring in the courtroom when he replied in a very dry humor, "Well the lines were very long." Again, Quinn was taking his words out of context. What he said was, " there was a time in the sixties when a person could tell about a persons character by the way he dressed, tattoos he wore, and such. In this day and age, it is extremely difficult however, because many of these things are now fashion statements. Unless a person is severely impaired, it is harder to visually determine problems by appearance alone."

Much of Dr. Dietz testimony focused on volitional control. He stated that even though a Paraphilic is impulsive to some extent, they still have control over their behavior. Unless, they are acting as a "wild beast," and do not monitor their behavior in the presence of authority. He described Sanchez as very cold, calculating and methodical in his planning. He described the lack of volitional control as this: If the person would continue to perform the behavior if a policeman were at his elbow. For this reason, he felt Sanchez had volitional control, and not showing any mental incapacity. He described his condition as one that a person does not chose to have but that the behavior is chosen. He admitted that alcohol and anger play a part in a persons control over their emotions. He also felt that Sanchez' relationship with Luz was a major part of his emotional upheaval. She gave him many mixed messages and he reacted to her in a very irrational manner. "If he did this behavior with each and every relationship he had, then the case for Borderline Personality Disorder would be stronger," he explained. Dietz believed that Sanchez did have volitional control of his behavior.

Dr. Dietz' theory regarding the reason Sanchez had the AK-47 in his truck that night was: to scare Luz, to shot Luz and then himself, to create drama, or to threaten to kill himself in front of her. The last being the story Sanchez told the doctor was his motive. Dr. Dietz does not believe that Sanchez planned to shot Megan, only to stop her.

At the end of Dr. Dietz testimony, the Prosecution asked to have his report entered into evidence. The Defense argued this point. Judge Riley stated they would discuss this outside the jury. What else was in that report that the Defense did not want us to see?

Footnote* John Hinckley, was found to be insane and has spend the past twenty years incarcerated in Psychiatric care. He shot President Ronald Reagan and missed his heart by two inches. His bullet did permanently injury the President's Press Secretary, Jim Brady, who now has paralysis and is confined to a wheelchair. Ironically, this week, Hinckley is eligible for parole consideration.

PROSECUTION'S REBUTTAL

The Prosecution ended its' rebuttal with two more witnesses. First was, Lori Pearlman, a psychiatric technician for the Forensic Medical Group at Ventura County Jail. Her responsibilities were to interview, assess psychiatric needs for medication and suicide interventions. She spoke with Sanchez about his history of suicide ideation. He stated that he had thought about suicide but would never do it. He also talked about his fathers' abusive nature toward his mother and siblings. Sanchez told Ms. Pearlman, "He did not get abused by his dad because he was the favorite-- the youngest."

Mrs. Schwartz, a resource counselor for the Simi Valley High School District brought records from Royale High where Sanchez attended. Vincent Sanchez had gone through the tenth grade but dropped out near the end of the school year. He had many absences, excused, unexcused, partial days attended, truancy and medical appointments that reflected poor attendance. His grades were a C and D in wrestling. He did enroll in the following school year, which would have been his eleventh grade, but was dropped by November for poor attendance. That semester, he had an A in wrestling but D's and F's in his other courses. So much for the good student that the Defense tried to portray. It seems that Sanchez may have exaggerated his future career in wrestling, as well.

The Prosecution asked to have a Newspaper article regarding the motorcycle accident published into evidence, but the Defense objected. So with that, the Prosecution rested their rebuttal.

DEFENSE' REBUTTAL

The Prosecution re-opened their rebuttal for one more witness today. Deputy Artera, the officer who escorted Sanchez from the courtroom after the guilt phase of his trial. He conversed with Sanchez, asking him what happened in court. Sanchez stated that he was found to be guilty. The deputy asked, "What happens next?" Sanchez told him, "They have the penalty phase. All I need is for one juror to feel sorry for me." He is right. All the jurors have to agree on the penalty before Judge Riley can sentence him to death.

The Defense opened their rebuttal with only one witness. Dr. Pablo Stewart, a psychiatrist. He has approximately twenty years in the field, as well as expertise in the area of Substance Abuse, Dual-Diagnosis (Mentally Ill who also have Substance Abuse issues), and Forensics. He reviews Appellate Court cases that involve the death penalty, when there is question of a Mental Disorder. It appeared that his sole purpose was to discredit Dr. Park Dietz, however. He stated that he disagreed with most of Dr. Dietz' testimony. But when asked to give examples, he replied that he could not remember specific comments. He felt that Dr. Dietz over simplified the case of Sanchez, and that he tended to view the situation in a black or white/ all or nothing fashion. When challenged by Dobroth about taking statements out of context, he just repeated that he did not commit all of Dr. Dietz testimony to memory. I wondered why he did not ask to view Dietz' report to clarify his statements. Dr. Stewart was asked, isn't Dr. Dietz well known and well respected in his field? Dr. Stewart stated, "He is well known but in my opinion, not well respected." He gave vague reasons; such as we travel in the same circles and talk with many of the same colleagues. Dobroth began to read parts of Dr. Dietz' credentials and all the while asking if Dr. Stewart knew this about him. Dr. Stewart responded by saying, "I do now." Finally, Dobroth stated, "Well, I don't intent to read all sixty-two pages of this," to which Dr. Stewart replied, "thank you." It seemed to me that there was some professional jealousy involved in Dr. Stewart's opinions. He remarked sarcastically, "Dr. Dietz is a good businessman and a self-promoter." He continued by saying, "No wonder he has to ask so much for his services. If he is doing all that his credentials say he is, he does not have time to do much else." If Dr. Dietz were present in the courtroom, I wonder if Dr. Stewart would have talked about him in this manner. I did not like the fact that he kept looking at the jury and smiling during these comments.

Dr. Stewart testified that he has never heard of the "police at the elbow test." (A rational person is less likely to commit a crime if police are present.) He felt that this was absurd! He also felt that Paraphilia and Personality Disorders do impair a persons' volitional control. So do anger or alcohol. He continued to say that simple things, like not eating a good breakfast will alter our blood sugar, and can impair our judgment. He stated that the Diagnostic Services Manual (DSM) is not the Bible, just a means of organizing conditions for the medical community. Dobroth tore into him, "are you aware that Dr. Dietz helped to write the DSM? Did you help write any of it?" Of course, he had not. Dr. Stewart did not offer much in the way of his own opinions. His focus was on disagreeing with the opinions of Dietz. He did not review any of Sanchez'childhood, victim's information, police reports, the videotapes, or any other pertinent information to this case. Mostly, he spoke of his review of Dr. Dietz' report and opinions. I later learned that not many jurors were impressed with Dr. Stewart.

The final procedures were to submit into evidence by stipulation that the motorcycle accident had happened to Sanchez, October 1986. Stipulation means both sides do not dispute. Judge Riley commented that this may be the one and only time they agree.

We then learned that Sanchez had lied when he stated he drew the five pencil drawings that were viewed by the jurors last week. He had another inmate at county jail draw them for him. I wonder how Ted felt? And how the Defense team felt when they learned that Sanchez had once again misrepresented himself. With this, the Defense rested their rebuttal.

Judge Riley read the Jury Instructions for the penalty phase. They were not nearly as long or complicated as the trial instructions. The Judge then advised us that the Prosecution would began closing arguments beginning with Mrs. Corona.

PROSECUTION CORONA'S CLOSING ARGUMENT

Prosecutor Dee Corona began her closing argument explaining the rules on aggravated and mitigating circumstance. She expressed that she would be spending most of her time talking about mitigating circumstances. The Prosecution had a photo display board of all of Sanchez' victims, including Curstain Conrad (the baby), Margy and Megan, fifteen in all. Mrs. Corona stated that once you reflect on all the persons who were harms by this defendant, it was more in the range of seventy-five people. There are the parents of each victim, sisters and brothers, grandparents, friends, and boyfriends or husbands. Corona stated that mitigating circumstances took into account Sanchez' school, jobs, friends, family and character. Then she began to break them down into detail. Corona says that the court evidence shows that Sanchez did not have a lack of ability in school, but that he had poor attendance. She reminded us that there was no proof that Sanchez was being scouted for his wrestling skills, only his reporting of that. As a matter of fact, he had C's and D's in wrestling in the tenth grade. When he came back to school the next semester, he received an A in wrestling, but had D's and F's in his other courses. She pointed out that he did wrestle after his motorcycle accident. Yet, he portrayed that his accident was supposed to have ended his hopes of a career in wrestling.

Ms. Corona stated that Sanchez' employment career was not much better. He had about three employers in a ten to fifteen year period, which resulted in his brother, Anthony paying most of his bills. Also, Sanchez had attempted to defraud Workmen's Compensation for thirty million, for the accident that occurred at the construction site.

Regarding his family and friends, Corona stated, "Of course, they want him to live." But she reminded us that many of his friends did not even know the real Vincent Sanchez. The family had reported differing ideas about their home life. Some remembered Vincent getting beaten and some did not, but rather as being one of the favored children of Mariano. Vincent told a Psychiatric Technician at the county jail that his dad did not abuse him because he was the favorite child. Mrs. Corona pointed out that this information was voiced before Sanchez ever was faced with the possibility of the death penalty. "So, was the dad really bad or just trying to control a house full of children?"

Prosecutor Corona explained to the jury that law in California does automatically allow for appeal on the death penalty but our jury instructions state that whatever sentence we give, we should assume that it will be carried out. Corona was very upset with the treatment that Defense Attorney Quinn had given Dr. Dietz. She stated that he was disrespectful and rude to Dr. Dietz while on the stand, so was Dr. Pablo Stewart during his testimony. She continued, "Dr. Dietz gets the money he does because he is the very best in his field." Corona expressed, "Dr. Dietz does not have simple-minded opinions, but cuts to the chase and is straightforward." Corona reviewed the three diagnoses of Dietz, Phenix and Adams. She reminded us that Dr. Dietz stated that not all persons with a Paraphilia are criminals, but rather choose to disregard the law and the rights of others. Corona felt that the experts' testimony explained why the Prosecution believed that Sanchez <u>did</u> have volitional control of his actions.

Then, she said, "I want to review with you the character of Mr. Sanchez by showing a few short clips of the rape scenes that he videotaped." You could feel a group sigh as we knew what we were in for. After seeing these tapes the first time, I wondered if I could ever get the images out of my head. Now, these images were going to be renewed. It was so upsetting to watch but I understood why the Prosecution requested that we do. They wanted to remind us how extensive the damage was to Sanchez' victims. A picture does speak a thousands words. At the conclusion of the videotapes, Mrs. Corona accented her scenario with, "This is the <u>real</u> Vincent Henry Sanchez." The jury filed out of the courtroom with none of our usually communication. I was on the verge of sobbing, but managed to get to my car before expressing it.

DEFENSE ATTORNEY HELFRICH CLOSES

Defense Attorney Helfrich began her closing statement with a quote from Gandhi. "An eye for an eye just leaves the whole world blind." I truly enjoy her speaking style as she has the ability to engage you in her thoughts. Helfrich thanked the jury for our continued sense of humor. I was glad to hear this. At times I felt that maybe some didn't think we were taking the whole thing serious enough. She was right when she stated that humor is a must in a case of this nature. Ms. Helfrich became teary-eyed when speaking of being involved with her client and this case for two years. She reminded us some of the reactions of the friends and family of Vincent Sanchez. Ted Sebodoa, who became emotional when he spoke about loving Vincent like a son. Shannon Stout, Jeanie Moak, Carmen Sanchez, Jeff Sullivan to name a few, who loved Vincent and felt he added to their lives, and had been a strong support for them when they needed it. Helfrich reminded us, "Vincent had many jobs in his lifetime. Jobs that had been overlooked by the Prosecution." She reminded us of the qualities that others saw in Vincent; hardworking, supportive, funny, active, and wanting to be involved like a family member. Ms. Helfrich inquired, "Do you think it is a coincidence that Vincent always hung out with other peoples' families? He wanted to be a part of something."

Then, she began going through the life history of Vincent, showing photographs of him as a child. His mother had described him as, "A happy, beautiful child that was all boy." Helfrich read some of the remarks that teachers of Vincent had made about him while in school. "He was social, sometimes talked too much, capable, and had a good sense of humor." Then she asked, "What happened to that happy, beautiful child?" The testimony of various sisters and brothers was repeated to express the cruelty and abuse in the Sanchez home. "How many of you hit your young boys in the stomach to discipline them? How many of you have watched as your mother was beaten, knocked unconscious, or had a finger broken? How many of you have had your father choke you when upset with you?" Ms. Helfrich was very upset that the Prosecution had minimized the treatment in the Sanchez home. "Why did the boys, Andrew and Frankie leave home at age fourteen? Anthony left and joined the marines at seventeen. Why did the children want to leave that household, if it was so good?"

Jan Helfrich reviewed the results of the Kaiser study regarding brain imprinting. The areas were sexual, physical, emotional, parental abuse, domestic violence, parental substance abuse, and a parent in prison. Results of the study revealed that a person growing up in this environment will most likely have depression, a substance abuse problem and be sexual promiscuous. She reminded us that Dr. Adams said that about ten per cent of all persons who were sexually abused, would become sexual offenders. (I would guess that the number is probably higher.) Vincent Sanchez did not have an ideal childhood by any means. And it is not a stretch to see how his experiences may have altered the personality he grew into.

That evening I wept for all the damage that was done to Vincent. And for all children receiving unfair treatment by the very people whom they trust and expect to care for them.

CHIEF PROSECUTOR DOBROTH'S CLOSING

Prosecutor Lela Dobroth began her closing statement, fiery as usual. She told the jury, "Don't be mad at us for showing you the rape tapes again. The reason we did is because we know that this is the last time we will be allowed to talk with you. We want you to remember why this defendant in here today." Dobroth stated this defense is the "abuse excuse to the max!" "Maybe many of you have had some of the same life experiences. Many of us in this room could have had a father that was a drunk. But it is no excuse to take the life of a young girl! No excuse to rape and harm all of these young women. Mr. Sanchez is a baby beater, sexual molester, and a murderer! The Defense describes Mr. Sanchez to you as a caring person. Was he caring about his mother, his sisters, or his family when he went out and stalked and rapes all these young girls? His family is suffering pain because of all of this, but he is the one who brought that pain on his family." She expressed concern that Mr. Quinn would be the last to speak with us, and described him as eloquent and bright.

Ms. Dobroth reminded us about the last witness, Deputy Artera who escorted Sanchez back to jail after his trial. Sanchez told the deputy that it only would take one juror to feel sorry for him. "Which one of you will be that one person who feels sorry for this defendant, she inquired? One of the ways that you, the jury can approach this tasks is to go back into the jury room and make a list of the things that Mr. Sanchez can add to society. I encourage you to talk about what contributions he can make. I suggest that the conversation will be a very short one."

Next, photographs were shown of Megan at various ages, and Dobroth repeated some of what her parents shared with the court. Again it was painful to hear their expressed grief and disbelief that their only daughter was gone. The impact on family and friends that Megan would never be able to walk on the beach, see the sky, laugh with her family, or share events in their lives. "But if Mr. Sanchez lives, he will be able to do some of these things," she concluded.

Then, Dobroth spoke about baby Curstain. She sighed, "But for the grace of God, Curstain would be dead now too." The doctors testified that she had subdural brain injury and retinal hemorrhage in both eyes. These injuries were consistent with a severe shaking and being beaten on the top of the head, not from a fall off the kitchen counter! Experts told us that a child that was in a car accident and thrown ten feet through the air would not suffer that type of injury. Evidence proved that Curstain had repeated injuries, as well." This is one of the most disturbing parts of this whole story to me. I cannot see how anyone can hurt a child in this manner. It makes the concept of mercy for this defendant much harder.

CHIEF DEFENSE ATTORNEY QUINN'S CLOSING

Defense Attorney Quinn began his closing statement by thanking the Prosecution for the kind words regarding his communication skills. He stated, "I am afraid that I am not up to this. Nothing prepares you for a moment like this." Quinn surprised us by stating, "My client is a pathetic loser!" I guess that the reason for this is so we believed that he was not making excuses for Sanchez' behavior. He stated that there is no excuse for murder. Quinn also instructed us that there is no automatic death penalty when a murder has been committed. That is why we were chosen to hear this case and decide. "The death penalty and life in prison are both punishment, just differing degrees of it," he informed us. But he argued the case for life in prison without the possibility of parole, (LWOPP as he called it.) He related to us that if we recommended Life, he would still be getting punished for his crime, and would not be able to hurt anybody else. Quinn suggested that Sanchez showed responsibility by admitting to his crimes and his being alive will allow the victims a chance to have a future dialogue with him, if they should choose to. Quinn explained that many times after a defendant gets through the court procedures, he begins to talk about his crimes and gains some insight into why he did what he did. Victims may want to confront the perpetrator for closure in their lives. If he spends his life in prison, he will be giving up control and power and not getting a free ride, as many may think. Quinn described Sanchez' admission of guilt to the sex crimes as a way to avoid having the victims come to court and deal with all their emotions again. And waiving his right to an appeal was a means of saving the Prosecution a lot of time and effort. Life in prison would also allow the people that love him to continue to have a relationship with him. Quinn stated, "Mercy illuminates the human soul." Quinn is much more compelling when he is speaking from the heart than when he is trying to educate us in the law. But he did resort to that again in this presentation by reading to us what some of the mitigating factors are. He spent most of his time on the K factor which is basically all other factors that impact this case, such as Sanchez' life history.

Neil Quinn called our attention to the tie he was wearing today. He says it is his "lucky tie." It was a picture of Vincent Van Gogh's Iris's. He explained when he had seen the painting as a young man, it brought him to tears. He still was not sure why, just that it was a human quality. I was not sure why he shared this with us, maybe to humanize himself to us. Or attempt to say that one does not always know why we do or feel the way we do. Maybe he was attempting to connect Vincent to Van Gogh, painter of beautiful pictures.

"What prepares a person to kill," Quinn asked? He shared that the only time we are ever prepared to kill is in the event that our own life is threatened, or we are going to war. One of the ways that young men are readied for going into battle is by de-humanizing the opponent. Another way is to give distance to the kill, or not put a face on it. Like dropping a bomb from afar. Quinn cautioned us not to "split" or just see the bad side of Vincent Sanchez. "As far as redemption, well, I don't know about redemption," states Quinn. Redemption in Webster's Dictionary means: a buying back, being redeemed, release from sin, to pay off or atone for. How does Vincent Henry Sanchez atone for his sins?

DELIBERATION OF THE SENTENCING PHASE

Deliberation for Vincent Sanchez began on Tuesday, following the Labor Day weekend. Many of the jurors labored with their thoughts during this break from court.

I spent time walking my dog and mulling the facts over in my mind. By the end of the weekend, I was convinced what my decision would be. But, I needed to hear what the others thought. I halfway hoped that they would convince me that I was wrong.

When we convened that morning, I asked if everyone would be willing to take a straw vote before we began discussing the case. The reason for this was to see just how effective the attorneys had been in presenting their case. By no means did I feel this would be the final vote. Everyone but one agreed to express their vote. It was six for death, five undecided, and one who chose not to say. Later, he explained that he had felt death was appropriate but wanted to hear what others felt. This demonstrated to us that both sides had done a good job and that our decision would not be a hasty one.

We began our task by reading the Aggravating and Mitigating jury instructions and pulling out the factors that applied in this case. Aggravating Factors were the death of Megan, other criminal behaviors that he was not charged with toward Luz and Anna, (one of the victims that was not names in the rape crimes), included all the rapes, kidnap, threatening of the rape victims, and the child abuse of Curstain. Last but not least was the long-lasting impact on all the victims of his crimes, including family and friends.

Mitigating Factors we were to consider were his mental or emotional disturbance, any Mental Disease or Intoxication. We were to review any aspects of his character, abuse history, possible sexual abuse, family dysfunction, school, work, and his contributions to society.

After listing all the factors that we should consider, we began at the top of our list to discuss the aggravating factors. These factors were things that added to the severity of his crimes. Mitigating factors were things that helped to explain his behavior or allow him consideration. At the end of this day, we stopped at Illumination of Character. We had a list of three things: sense of humor, work ethic, and positive role model for his nephews. Prosecutor Dobroth would have gotten a chuckle from this list.

AFTER DELIBERATION

After deliberating the sentence for a day and a half, we decided to stop and sleep on it. One of the jurors had a major test the following day and needed time to focus on it so we all took this time to reflect on the information we had before us. Thus far we had discussed: the impact on all the victims, their families and friends, Sanchez' dysfunctional family life, his purposeful actions, his mental state (evil, insane, or criminal?), how we felt about the death penalty, Sanchez' remorse or lack of, his resistance to treatment or help, expert opinions vs. our opinions, and the possibility of sexual abuse of Sanchez. We debated the degrees of each aggravating factor and the degrees of mitigating factors. Just how much weight do you put on his crimes while regarding his past life experience? I did my homework the night before, which was to make a list of the positive aspects of Sanchez'character, as well as the negative aspects. We must keep in mind that nobody is all-bad! I presented my list to the jurors the following day and they seemed to feel the evaluation was both appropriate and comprehensive. The problem being, we felt the negative side almost doubled the positive side. We discussed the positive qualities we had heard witnesses say about him. Such as his sense of humor, being a hard worker, encouraging to family children, good with Andrew (Luz' downs syndrome child), helpful, dependable, emotionally supportive, caring, trustworthy, competitive, social, handy, and he had shown some remorse toward Luz and shame for the pain he had caused his family.

Sanchez has a negative side also. It consists of dark moods, financially dependency, emotional and physical abuse to baby Curstain Conrad, jealousy for attention, self-serving, manipulative, deceitful/lair, cold and calculating, little emotion for others pain, controlling, blaming others for his short comings, minimizing his behaviors, criminal thinking ("I'll get by with whatever I can"), defrauding, sexual predatory behavior, anger control issues, substance abuse issues, poor self-esteem/bragger, thief, possessiveness, and lack of remorse for his victims. None of us saw much evidence of remorse toward these women!

When we came back on Thursday, September fourth, we took another vote. Everyone had come to the same decision. We went around the room and asked everyone to give their final thoughts about this case. Then we signed the jury form and rang for the bailiff. He gave the verdict to Judge Riley, who sent word that it would be approximately forty-five minutes before everyone could be assembled in the courtroom for the reading of the sentence.

Upon entering the courtroom, we could see that the room was full of people; many whom we had never seen before. We later learned that they were staff of the Prosecution and Defense, who had worked hard on this case for almost two years and had vested interest in it's outcome. The saddest thing was that the parents of Sanchez had not arrived before the sentence was read. They were seen coming into the building as many of us were leaving.

I hoped that the reporters did not approach them before the Defense had a chance to tell them the Sentence. The Judge requested that each one of the jurors state their response to the sentence. All twelve of us affirmed that we had agreed on the death penalty for Sanchez. He remained still and emotionless as the sentence was read. Most of the Attorneys hid their emotions with an expressionless face. The audience remained silent. The family of Megan held hands. The whole proceeding felt very surreal. Then Judge Riley thanked us again for our dedication to the case, and our time and patience. He informed us that we could speak about the case now, but could not receive any financial benefit from this case for at least ninety days following the sentence. He assured us that the press, any attorney or representatives would not contact us and our information files would be sealed to protect our privacy. But if we wanted to talk with the attorneys or press, we were now allowed to do so. As we filed out of the courtroom, the deputies assisted us to get our things and exit the courthouse without being accosted by the Press.

A few of the jurors met later at a watering hole near the courthouse and discussed our feelings. The press had managed to corner some of the jurors for comments as they left the building. Nobody wanted to talk to anybody outside our group at this point. We had been through a unique experience. An experience that we had not been able to share with our families or spouses. I liken it to war vets, who can only share their experience with other war vets. Now we could talk with our family and friends about the case. But could they truly relate to the stress we were under? Or the heavy burden required to look into a man's face and tell him his life was not worth saving? We are now free to discuss how this whole case has affected us for so many months. And how we came to the decision we did. The remainder of my evening was spent getting drunk and crying about this case. If only Sanchez would have accepted treatment. If only he had shown remorse for his victims. If only! I do not regret my decision but that did not make it any easier to make. Vincent Sanchez had gotten 180 days in prison for nearing beating a thirteen-month-old baby to death. He received life in prison for assaulting, terrorizing, and altering thirteen young women' lives forever. He deserved death for shooting Megan with an assault rifle, kidnapping and possible rape, and then dumping her body in a canyon.

I felt sad for the family and friends of Vincent Sanchez. I felt sad for the life that he had lived and the experiences he had been through. He was a product of an abusive household and poor role modeling. But most of all, I felt bad for the young ladies he abused. And for the small child who didn't have a chance, and nobody to protect her from his abuse. And I think of all the ways their lives will be altered forever. Lastly, I felt grief for the family of Megan. Their loved-one paid the ultimate price of Vincent's dysfunctional choices.

CLOSURE

The morning after the close of the sentence phase, I stumbled, sleepy-eyed into my bathroom. The orchid plant that had been dormant for months, was in full bloom with a beautiful white and purple orchid. I began to cry, remembering what Art Barroso had said about Megan reminding him of a beautiful orchid just starting to bloom into her life.

After the trial, I went to visit the monument for Megan that was placed on the previous Camarillo State Hospital grounds. After much searching, I found it in a quiet little courtyard off the main mall. A jacaranda tree was planted there, a wooden bench and a plaque. I placed a white orchid next to the plaque that read:

Be aware. Be careful.

Look out for each other.

In memory of Megan Barroso
1981-2001

California State University Channel Islands

At the close of this chapter, my hope is that there will be some closure and healing for all the families involved. My hope for this planet is that we will stop hurting each other by poisoning our relationships with anger and violence.

Vincent Henry Sanchez has poisoned many lives with his actions. May God have mercy on his soul.

SENTENCING DAY FOR PENALTY PHASE

Tuesday, November 4, 2003 was the formal sentencing of Vincent Sanchez. It took twenty minutes to seat the courtroom. Many people waiting outside the courtroom had to be sent away. Deputy Bailiff, Abbott gave eight jurors on this case special consideration and seated us in the back. It might seem strange to some, that so many jurors would return for the sentencing in this case, but we had invested much time and emotion into this case and it served as closure for us. The family and friends of Megan thanked us for our hard work and for our time away from our own families. I must say that all through the process, I felt we were appreciated and shown respect by the courtroom personnel, the family and friends of the victims, the victims themselves, and the Sanchez family. Judge Riley was always very respectful of us and sent us letters of appreciation for our patience and dedication to this process. I did not feel that we were ever the "forgotten persons" that he alluded to, that sometimes happens in a case like this.

Chief Defense Attorney, Quinn made a statement to the court regarding why the sentence should not continue at this time. It was unclear to us when he stated that it was not within the courts powers to make the findings in this case, and that it failed to address any mitigating circumstances. Chief Prosecuting Attorney, Dobroth disagreed with both statements, and referred to statements made by Dr. Phenix and the Sanchez family testimony that had addressed these circumstances. It seemed that this was just an attempt to postpone the inevitable. Apparently Judge Riley did not agree with Quinn because he proceeded by making a statement that due to the complex nature of this case, only statutory statements of victim impact would be heard. This meant that several of the friends of Megan would not be allowed to share their prepared statements to the court. For this reason, I later offered to include them in this book.

Suzan Barroso, Megan's mother spoke first. This is her statement:

"Everyone suffers loss of family and/or friends at some time in life, but through the tragedy of my daughter Megan's death, I have a sadness that will color my outlook on life until the day I die. I ache for the terror and pain she must have felt, when she realized that she was going to die that night in July of 2001. I have anguished, recurring imaginations of how she he died and laid for so long in that canyon undiscovered. I also have wasted feelings of disgust and anger toward the defendant. Even now, it's difficult to separate the sorrow I feel for <u>my</u> loss, my regret for what <u>Megan</u> lost, and looking through her eyes, the terror, possible agony, and the total violent obliteration of her life. I have been lucky so far; I haven't suffered physical or debilitating emotional trauma as a result of the crime against Megan, just a sadness that never leaves.

Regarding **isolation and loss**: Megan's death reflects increased isolation for my son and myself. I have lost dreams for Megan and me. I have been socialized to believe that all accomplishments in my life pale in comparison to raising happy, healthy, socially responsible, insightful and productive children. I have been robbed of my only daughter and feel the devastating loss of a child more acutely than had we been an intact family. We had a bond that exists only between mother and daughter. Her life as an adult showed promise. Megan was **half** of my immediate family. Her brother A.J. was the other half. Megan, A.J. and I were isolated from the rest of my family because most of them lived in other states, but we managed to see my parents and sister infrequently through the years.

Memories, a blossoming young woman and dreams of the future

Of course I have many memories of Megan growing up, but as she grew, both she and I talked about her future. I will never get over not having the adult daughter I used to dream of when Megan was a little girl and feel cheated that I won't get to finish raising her – and I know raising children extends <u>long</u> past the age of 18. She was only 20 years and 3 months – not old enough to do many things that adults 21 and over, take for granted. She will never be able to feel emotions, especially the exhilaration of accomplishment, and never have a family of her own. It hurts to think that I may never have grandchildren.

Megan presented as any other fun loving 20-year-old girl, anxiously seeking to prove her independence. I value the characteristics of self-sufficiency and independence and have raised my children to value it also. When the going seemed especially tough for

Megan, I reminded her that she could always come home to be a full time student – something she said she wanted. Her response was that when she looked around her apartment - she felt a sense of pride from having earned her own money to pay the rent, buy a used refrigerator, pay half of the utilities, and purchase her own clothes and food. She stated, "Now that I've had a taste of independence, I don't want to give it up." (Hearing her say that was a "Proud Mom moment".)

Regarding the promise she began to show as a young adult, Megan was starting to develop a curiosity about religion and philosophy, as evidenced by the weekly Bible studies she attended in Newbury Park and the books she had begun reading before her death. Our plan was to have her complete two years of general education units at Moorpark while I finished the two-year Masters in Social Work program at Fresno. At the completion of her two years, she planned to transfer to a four-year school, probably Cal State Channel Islands, Cal State Fresno, or Cal Poly San Luis Obispo. She wasn't sure of her vocation, but she leaned toward a human services profession. After her death, I was wistfully reminded of her every time I saw a young woman that resembled her in age and appearance on campus. I would have given anything to have her be the one going to classes, hearing the bells chime hourly, and having fun with her friends. I used to imagine us discussing issues of daily concern that mothers and daughters do, as well as discussing movies, books, our work, and social issues.

Impact of Megan's brother – A.J.

I am concerned about how the tragedy of Meagan's death will affect my son. A.J. will never have his sister to share the joys and sorrows that life will bring him, and Mr. Sanchez' actions have not helped the emotions of a young man **trying so hard** to grow up with a positive outlook on life. I hope he hasn't done irreparable harm to the psychological health of Megan's brother. An apology from the defendant is lame, at best.

A.J. does not yet see the impact of his sister's death on him because he is still hurt by the sibling rivalry between him and Megan during their childhood. As he matures, A.J. will miss the sister he lived with while he grew up and feel the same aching loss I do. A.J. has not expressed the need for counseling. When he begins to fully realize the potential his adult relationship with his sister could have meant for him, he may encounter an overwhelming realization of the support they could have given each other in meeting life's challenges.

Personal impact

Although I know anger can be positive, just now I see it as a wasted emotion. It's not fair that I should expend such energy because of the murderous assault on my daughter. I am **disgusted** not only at what has been done to Megan and the other victims, but that the defendant dared to make excuses for his behavior. In my mind he should receive the same punishment he gave Megan – and in the same manner.

I wonder if at some point as she was being terrorized or dying, if Megan cried out for me – just as she often did in times of trouble. Did she suffer much before she died? Megan, like the other Sanchez victims, was *not* engaging in risky behavior – unless going home late at night – sober - is risky.

Parents warn their children about the consequences of indulging in risky behavior. Megan was sensible about her behavior and the company she kept. It is difficult to accept that no matter how well children are trained to avoid potentially bad situations or people, they can be in the wrong place at the wrong time – and become the victim of a predator. If I was younger, I would be afraid to have more children, fearing he or she could easily fall prey to someone claiming to have a mental or personality disorder. Fortunately, Megan's killer was caught, but unfortunately for other parents and grandparents, predators still stalk and attack. I wonder how any parent concerned for their child's welfare could ever have compassion for some one who would so viciously attack and murder a helpless and innocent young woman; yet there are people who make excuses for predators, rapists and murderers. I am not one who makes excuses for them. Recently I declined the opportunity to work with the Sexually Violent Predator population as a clinician at my employment.

A.J. and I have been robbed by Megan's death. I'm lucky if an hour goes by when I don't think about her, yearn for her presence, review the "if only" scenarios, and reflect on the terrible way she died. Waves of disbelief that she is gone wash over me less frequently now. Friends and other therapists have told me that the harshness of the initial wound would soften, but never go away. So far, they're right.

I am glad the jury has recommended the death penalty for Mr. Sanchez, however the death penalty would be more meaningful to surviving victims and those that believe in a death penalty if the time between sentencing and execution was no longer than the appeal process for prisoners with other kinds of sentences. Unfortunately, death penalty prisoners get special treatment and privileges, many more appeals than other prisoners, and in California the length of time that elapses between sentencing and execution is many years. One appeal seems enough, when so much time and money is expended proving the defendant's guilt beyond doubt. (In the days before DNA testing the time and money involved was more justified.)

It seems fair that Mr. Sanchez should have **no** human contact and privileges. Since he condemned Megan from having life; I would ask that he not be allowed to socialize with other prisoners, prison personnel and have **no** creature comforts. If he never saw the sun, sky or grass until he is executed, Megan's brother A.J. and I would be happier still.

Restitution

Megan had no life insurance and the cost of funeral expenses were not totally reimbursed to me by the Victim's Compensation Fund. I kept an accounting of the money she owed me, because I advised her to pay her other debts before she paid me.

Except for $1, 047.76 for burial expenses yet to be reimbursed, and $650 for gas and lodging expenses to travel to Ventura County these past two years, it is not my wish to be further reimbursed expenses by the state. I feel the burden of restitution (beyond funeral and travel expenses) should lie with the prisoner who is directly responsible for my daughter's death. Ideally, Mr. Sanchez would work while in prison – to pay off the other itemized expenses – Megan's debts to me. ($3,450.90)

I am aware that prisoners and families try to manipulate the system to minimize their financial and moral responsibilities to victims once in a correctional facility. I ask the court for guidance and intervention to *not allow* this to happen.

Financial responsibility

I am requesting that at least some financial restitution be directly borne by the prisoner, with the maximum allowable percentage by law to be garnished monthly from his account in prison, until the entire amount of Megan's debt is paid. I further request that no transfer of funds from Mr. Sanchez's prison accounts be made to another person or persons – or other inmates until the maximum percentage of the garnishment is met – for the entire month.

I also request that Mr. Sanchez not receive candy, snacks or tobacco while prison, whether from prison programs or through outside sources.

It is my hope that the many other victims of Mr. Sanchez will seek financial restitution from him. (It is galling to think that he might be able to sit in prison and enjoy purchases from the prison canteen, while he viciously deprived my daughter of her life and psychologically damaged so many others.)

Moral responsibility

I ask that special attention be given to Mr. Sanchez' *possibility* of malingering regarding his mental health. It is my understanding that many prisoners feign signs and symptoms of a mental illness in order to get sent to special housing units or a treatment facility that will allow them to serve a pleasanter, easier sentence.

Respectfully, Suzan Barroso

Megan's aunt, Susie spoke next. (I am paraphrasing the following three statements). "I remember her as a little girl, always happy and playful. I have a favorite picture of her as a child, smelling a flower. I was very proud of Megan and respected her for her independence at such a young age. She chose to help a friend and it cost her life."

The last sexual assault victim (I called Donna) spoke about writing a thesis about the death penalty when she was in High School. She stated, " The funny thing is, I still feel the same way about it as in did back then. I suffer from survivor's guilt. Guilt that I survived and Megan died. I lock my doors five to six times a night. I have serious intimacy and relationships issues. I don't date now. I developed an addiction to pills and alcohol following my attack. I lost my job, still have nightmares, and had serious interpersonal problems with my mother for a while. I had a seizure at my job, due to fear and anxiety, and still suffer from panic attacks. I now have a prejudice against Hispanics. This defendant does not have any remorse for what he did to Megan because he picked me off the street only five days after she killed her and dumped her body."

The victim prior to Megan (I call Annette,) also made a statement. She asked Judge Riley if she could stand during her statement, to which he affirmed. "I choose to stand, because I can stand! I am standing for Megan! I am standing for all the victims of this man! He intended to torture, rape, and kill me. He videotaped the day at my house before he attacked me. And the problem is, he is one of many of his type. He bound and tied me. After spending hours with him, I know this man! All of us, who spent time with him, know him. He is not mentally ill! I know mental illness. This man has ruined many lives. Annette continued with a feverish tone. I am appalled at the Defense trying to make me the bad person. I am a doctor today. I passed the board second in my class. It was possible through a lot of hard work, because I could not even say the word "blue" for about two months after my attack. I was the victim before Megan and I too, feel guilty that there were others after me. I do not wish the defendant to be tortured or raped in prison, as none of this will take back what has happened. He is sick, like anyone who gets his "jollies" by hurting others. My father still cries because he was not there for me. I sleep with a hammer next to my bed and pity the next poor bastard who tries to come at me. I have written this speech at least 350 times over the past few years. It has ranged from, "I hope he rots in hell, to God bless him." Megan comes to me in spirit. Her spirit is strong. The Barroso family did not fail her. But I don't know about the Sanchez family."

"This is not Vincent Sanchez' judgment day. His judgment will come when he stands before the Lord. I told him I believed in Jesus and he left me that day, because he saw the Holy Spirit with me. I still have breathing issues and relationships issues. I have been with only one man since, and that was only so I would not have to be alone. What about these other young girls? I was 29 years old when I was attacked. They were much younger. How do these young girls form healthy relationships? I fled Simi Valley because he said he was coming back for me. My Dad saw him walking on my street, and this man ran when he realized he had been seen. I promise this court and all the people in it, that I will do a hundred times more good with my life than this man has done bad with his." Then Annette sat down, weeping.

It was good to witness the healing that was taking place this day in the courtroom-- victims of crime having a voice. Probably one of the most progressive steps the justice system has taken toward addressing violence in our society.

Lastly, Art Barroso spoke to the court. (Paraphrasing) "As you can imagine this whole ordeal has been a terrible nightmare for me. When the police came to my door early in the morning of July 5th, I only knew that Megan was not in her car and that a bullet hole had gone through the side door. Later, when I learned that the bullet hole was actually six holes with an AK-47, I knew Megan was in serious trouble. I still expected Megan to call me as she did when she needed help. Megan would call me."

"Over the course of the investigation, the police told me they could not tell me anything for fear of jeopardizing the case. It was very distressing to think that the police knew things that they could not tell me about Megan. Most of what I learned was through the reporters. For this reason, I took every opportunity to speak with them on Megan's behalf. When I would have time to myself, I sat in the dark and imagined the worst. I cried a lot but only to myself. Knowledge of the AK-47 took this whole nightmare into an even darker dimension because it made me re-live my nightmare of Vietnam over and over again. Up until July 5th, Nam had been the worst experience I had gone through in my life. Vietnam has been the source of thirty-two years of nightmares. For thirty-two years, I have worked through the fears and sadness of my Vietnam experience. Now, it all came flooding back. Megan was the same age as I was when I was faced with the threat of death by an AK-47. No child or young person should have to go through anything like this!"

"When I was twenty, Megan's age, I was an infantry soldier in Vietnam. In my first incident of combat, Viet Cong, firing AK-47's, ambushed the forward unit of our company. After the firefight, I watched as the dead lifeless bodies of my friends were dragged out of the battle area. The brutality of war and the devastation caused by the AK-47's struck me with so much shock, that it immediately altered my reality of life and death. The next day, my squad was informed that we would be the lead squad in patrolling the area of yesterday's attack. We traveled one hundred yards before being ambushed by AK-47 fire again. I fell to the ground where there was absolutely no cover, and laid there expecting to be killed. The AK-47 fire was only twenty-five yards away and I knew they had a clear shot. Petrified with fear, I felt an enormous sense of pity for myself. How could this happen? I was only twenty years old and about to die. The fact that Megan was attacked and killed by an AK-47 tortures my mind, body, and soul. In trying to give some meaning to the misery of war, I held onto the thought that what I went through would help save my children from ever going through it. I was wrong! The senseless cruelty and evil inflicted on Megan by this defendant, has left me with profound emotional and physical pain."

"Among the wonderful memories that I have of Megan was when she was about eight months old and I remembered racing home at lunchtime to see her. When she saw me, she would kick her little legs with excitement. And I would pick her up and hug her. The sweet smell of her as a baby stays etched in my mind and as a young lady I could still smell that sweet, clean smell when I held her. The thing I miss the most is being able to hug Megan. Now, my survival depends on my staying busy. I wanted to curl up in a corner and loose myself deep in depression, but I knew I had to survive for the rest of my family. One day, when I had a sharp pain to my chest, I felt I might be having a heart attack. But now I realize it was the pain of a broken heart."

"My memories of Megan are many. Her jumping up and down to Michael Jackson at three years old. Megan would ask my opinion about dating. I told her one time, "Megan, don't judge a man by his words but by his actions." Art's voice was flat and controlled, as he attempted to keep his emotions in check. But when one looked at him, you could see a broken man and a veil of sadness that covered him.

"Once when we argued, I asked her why she even came over if she felt this way toward me. Megan stated, because I love you dad! She had a beautiful soul and was loving even when she was angry with me. I remember at a family function recently, I watched her as she interacted with our family and thought Megan is a beautiful little girl who is growing into a charming young lady. Megan represented a huge investment in time, money and love that in the past few months, she repaid ten fold."

"Your Honor, I would like to start to heal from the horrendous emotional and physical pain this defendant has caused me and my family. But I cannot begin to heal until there has been an equitable punishment, sentence and retribution for the individual who caused all of this evil in the first place. How is it possible to show mercy? In my opinion, Sanchez has earned the death penalty with his barbaric acts against the women and children of this community. There are those who ask for compassion. But I feel their compassion is misdirected. There are other twisted minds like Sanchez, waiting to see if this community will hold him responsible and accountable for the atrocities he has committed. The Defense told the court about a letter of apology that Mr. Sanchez wrote to the Barroso family. It was not a letter of remorse. He stated that he was sorry for the pain that a trial would bring to us and intended to plead guilty for life in prison (to avoid getting the death penalty). He was right about the trial being painful. It was painful listening to the Defense minimize his actions. The Defense would have you believe that Megan was at fault for getting in the way of the defendant's spontaneous fit of rage. How ridiculous! And how insulting to the intellect of thinking people! And how so very painful to me. He and his defense team were upset that the Prosecution was not accepting a guilty plea from Sanchez, and instead of life in prison, intended to push for the death penalty. At times, this trial seemed to be more about providing Sanchez with a fair trial than about justice for Megan. He got his fair trial!"

In conclusion, "Your Honor, if I had the opportunity to talk to the defendant, I would say this. You have lived the life of a coward, hiding behind the powerful threats of guns and knives, to have your will with women and children. You now have the opportunity to do something like a man. By dying like one. Accept that your death sentence is a result of the barbaric acts that you committed. You lived like a coward…for once in your miserable life, do something like a man…and die like one!" The courtroom was completely silent as Art took his seat.

Before Judge Riley imposed the sentencing, Defense Attorney Quinn stated that Sanchez had a statement to make to the court.

Vincent Sanchez' statement (paraphrased): "I am willing to accept the death penalty and to take responsibility for the wrong that I have done. I just wish I had been caught sooner. Before I hurt all those people. To the sexual assault victims, I am sorry and hope that through the human process you can began to heal. To the jury, I am sorry that you had to go through all this for four months, seeing all those photos, and videos. I know it was not easy for you. I accept your verdict of guilty. To my Defense team, Mr. Quinn, Mrs. Helfrich, and Annette Town, who worked so hard on my behalf. You went above and beyond to help me. You have very big hearts, and I feel blessed to have had you as my team. To the Court, I apologize for all I put you through. The District Attorneys did a good job and I have no hard feelings toward you. Keep up the good job and continue to get people like me off the streets."

Then Sanchez read a poem he had written about Megan, called "Another Angel Leaves the Earth." (I attempted to get a copy of the poem to publish in my story but was unsuccessful in doing so). In the poem, he admitted that the bullet that night was supposed to be for him. I hoped that Vincent really felt what he said this day. Many people probably don't believe his did. Only the angels know if this will be the beginning of his redemption.

The rest of the afternoon was spent going through the mathematics of sentencing. It resulted in approximately 600 years in prison, if he does not die on death row. He was remanded to the Ventura County Sheriff's Department to be transported to San Quentin State Prison to await the appeal process. In California, the death penalty has an automatic appeal, and the average waiting period for death is about fourteen years.

BEST FRIENDS'
THOUGHTS

The following statement was given to me by one of Megan's best friends, Kimberly:

"I'm supposed to give an explanation of my reaction to the news of Megan's death. Like it really is possible. I'm not exactly an optimistic person. So I had a gut feeling she was dead or dying. Lying in a ditch somewhere, thinking of a Radiohead song or something. I also figured she was raped. I mean, she was a cross between Marissa Tomei and Snow White; ivory skin and big, soft brown eyes. I can't even imagine what those eyes saw that early morning, when all Megan wanted to do was take a quick shower and hit the pillow. I guess no one will ever know."

"Megan's death has done quite a number on me. I'm going through those stages of grief but I am still stuck on the first one. I think it is denial. I don't even know. Secretly, I pretend she is on vacation. I talk to her pictures. I kiss them. And she is the first star I see at night. I have all her phone numbers still programmed in my phone and I occasionally drive by her apartment, where I spent so many days and nights with her. There is a big hole in my heart now and it won't ever be filled. People ask me what will give me closure. My answer is simple. When I die, I will have closure. But I am working on that in therapy."

"I gained forty pounds after Megan was violently taken. So I didn't have the best self-esteem. I was really sad all the time after the shock wore off, and I wasn't numb anymore. I cried as much as I took a breath. It was so bad. My family didn't know what to do. Neither did I, so I took a lot of pills. I thought somehow Megan would come to me in my drugged stupor. But only charcoal...and hospitals...and doctors came my way. I don't believe in God anymore. Megan must be upset about that. But she has to understand my views on this. How a God could let such a good girl, pure in every way, be in the same vicinity with such an inferior, insecure, little loser?"

"I was told to write about the appropriate sentence for Vincent Sanchez. I have looked into medieval torture and although a lot of it sounds really good, it seems a little too tame. I want pain. And tears. Blood would be nice. Castration. I want him to feel what a virgin feels a million times worse."

"I have had a lot of friends in my life, but never anyone like Megan. She was different. She didn't take any bull from me and she told me like it was. You need people like that around. I try to visualize what she would be doing right now. I see her with a steady boyfriend, a big mucky-muck at Gramici where she worked. And us going out and dancing the night away like we used to do. Just being young, carefree girls."

"My first-born girl will be named Megan, and I know she would love that. She was going to be my kid's aunt. I dream about her all the time but I always wake up too soon. I always wake up feeling refreshed and happy. I miss her! Five minutes doesn't go by without me thinking of her. I don't understand why this happened. We never hung with anyone that was questionable or gave us reason to worry. Megan was really paranoid about people. She always took her own car so she could leave if she felt uncomfortable in a situation. But this situation she could not get out of."

It's ironic that her favorite song is called, "How To Disappear Completely Without Really Trying." I'll end with a quote from it---"That day, it's not me. I'll go where I please. I walk through walls, I float down. I'm laughing, I'm not here. This isn't happening."

The following is a statement by Megan's first girlfriend, Crickett:

"I can remember the first time I met Megan, back when we were both little girls. After a night of clogging, our mothers introduced us. I don't know why or how our mothers even knew each other, but that did not matter. We clicked instantly. That night, oddly enough, I can still remember exactly what Megan was wearing."

"It is funny to look back and remember my mother telling me to go sit by Megan because she thought we might make good friends. There was someone else with us that night, yet even with all the details I remember of Megan, I don't remember the other girl. Obviously, she was not anywhere near as important to me as Megan. I have learned that memories like that are made clear for many reasons. Not having Megan here with us today has obviously impacted my memories."

"Megan was always so alive and full of excitement. A kind of excitement you won't find in many people. Unfortunately, an excitement that now you won't ever be able to witness again, because HE robbed us of it."

"Since our clogging classes was held at my house, we would sit on my front lawn each week and have the funniest things to tell each other. Megan had the most wonderful sense of humor I had ever known."

"Our friendship blossomed for many years. We would talk on the phone for hours each day. After a while, one of our parents would tell us to get off the phone. Then we would argue over who would hang up first. Megan's spunkiness always rubbed off on me, and I wanted to be more like her. She was such an optimistic person. I think her optimism is what got her through many situations in life. But unfortunately, not this last one."

"Even though I had one sister at the time, Megan was truly just as close to me as any sister could be. Maybe even closer. We had that special thing where if we argued, we would only stay mad for maybe an hour. We couldn't wait long before calling each other to make up. Not having her in my life was something I never thought of, and now literally, not having her in my life is something I'm forced to think of. It is terrible what this man has done with his sick mind and body. An act that only wicked souls could complete."

"Throughout our lives, Megan and I were always on clogging teams together. She was very involved with the clogging community and was truly loved by all. Our dance team wrote a dance for our routine and still performs it today. First, as a tradition for the team, and secondly in Megan's memory. The dance is special to me because it came as a result of our friendship, which lives on today."

"When we reached High School, we were excited to find that we were in classes together. If we had not met five years ago through clogging, we were destined to meet each other at school. I would not want it any other way. Megan was my absolute best friend. We would often get into trouble with the teacher for laughing and giggling together. There seemed to be no controlling your laughter when Megan was around. She was one of those bubbly, contagious friends who brought out the best in people."

"When we weren't clogging, we would try to study but that seemed to be a lost cause. We'd end up talking for a long while before we even noticed we had gotten off track. I think that is one of the things I really loved about her. We could do crazy teenybopper things and we didn't have to worry about what the other person thought. We already knew what each other were thinking...literally! I have no one to share that special connection with now. Just myself, and the prayers I hold for her soul."

"The summer after our freshman year, Megan moved away. I was devastated. I didn't know what I was going to do without her. So we got the idea that it would be cool if she moved in with my family. I knew this could be possible, because my family often cared for kids who needed a place to stay. So Megan and I plotted. I asked my father if she could move in and he got on the phone to Suzan, her mother and verified that this was what we wanted. He knew how important Megan was to me, and that this was something that had to happen."

"So Megan moved in and I was living with my best friend. Or my new sister, I should say. We shared a room together, classes together, clogging together and our lives. It was great fun. She always added a positive feeling to the family. Megan never stopped smiling, that is for sure. In fact, it was a rare occurrence to see her hurt or upset. My family accepted her and all her great attributes to our household."

"These are memories that no one can take away from me. I look back on all that we have been through and know that even though Megan was brutally murdered, her loving spirit will always be with us. When we found out that Megan was missing, my heart broke. She was such a part of me, and because of her murder, I will have a void in my heart."

" I must say that after Megan moved out, we had a falling apart. And for quite some time, we really struggled with each other. Until one night, we sat down and talked about how we could re-build our relationship. We both had missed each other and longed to become close again. At that moment, I began to get excited about what our future would be. But then it came to a screeching halt. In fact, because of this perverted person, it was about to end. I had put my heart back into the relationship and was eager to start anew. The night we had talked was only a few days before Vincent Sanchez ended our opportunity for a friendship forever. I would never get the chance to talk with her or catch up on the years we had lost. I will never get to hear her tell any of the jokes that only we knew. Nor would I ever get to clog with her again."

"The entire clogging community knows Megan and remembers all the joy she brought them. Though Sanchez proved to be physically stronger than Megan, his soul is weak and broken, and he is full of hate. In the end, Megan proved to be the stronger person because her spirit still lives on through all of us. All will truly miss her. But mostly by me, her first true friend."

A.J.'S STATEMENT ABOUT MEGAN

Her brother A.J. did not have the same memories of Megan that other family and friends shared. Unfortunately, he remembers mostly bad times between he and Megan. He told me, "We were like oil and water." They argued a lot, as siblings sometimes do. But he felt that they really did not like one another. He remembers the last time they spent together was Thanksgiving, and they got into an argument because he did not want to disclose a situation between himself and a friend. He felt Megan was pushy and would not take no for an answer. When he and Megan argued, she would always call for her Mom. He related one time when this occurred he chimed in along with her, causing them all to laugh. A.J. felt Megan had a feeling of superiority over him, as well as others. He stated that she would berate him by calling him "a loser or a mistake."

When asked how he felt about Vincent Sanchez and what would he want to say to him, he replied, "he is a dumb shit Mexican. But on some level I can identify with him.

He didn't seem to like life, and I don't much like it either. He had a drinking problem and because I had issues with drinking, I can understand how he went down the path he did. I can identify with his anger. Life does not go easy for me, but I know that it is mostly my fault."

Asked if he felt guilty for not missing Megan, he replied, "At first, I asked myself why don't I feel guilty? But my Psychiatrist told me not to push it. Don't try to feel it just because others make you think you should." A.J. described Megan as "spoiled, mean, and hurtful. Nothing was ever good enough for her. She ruined everything for my mom and me. Megan wanted to be a makeup artist but she did not follow through with her schooling."

One of the things that brought he and Megan together was their suffering together. Their mom would have the neighbor care for them while she was out, and they were both afraid of the lady. A.J. describes her as crazy and weird. "She would make up stories that scared us, as well as tell our mom stories about us that were not true. I still have nightmares about that lady!"

When asked if he were quoted, what would he want to say about this whole episode of his life? He stated, "Whoever says they love America, has never been to California. They have dragged this trial out for twenty-nine months now. He was as guilty as hell, but it seems impossible to get the death penalty here!" When I commented to A.J. that he seemed real bitter, he stated, "I am just annoyed about what we have been put through."

Suzan Barroso had encouraged me to speak to A.J. and I must say I was surprised by what I heard. She and Art had both described him as a young man struggling to find his way. My impression is that he struggles with survivor guilt. Many times young people will feel guilty for remaining alive when someone they care for and see as better than themselves, does not live. They tend to sabotage their own success with unresolved feelings. At this point, A.J. is working to resolve his negative experiences with his sister.

AFTERMATH

After the court proceedings, I was able to make contact with Art and Susan Barroso.

Art was still struggling with various situations around the death of Megan. At his job, he requested to avoid a position change during the process of the trial because it was too stressful. In order to avoid the change, he was required to go to Employee Assistance and see a psychiatrist. Art was diagnosed with clinical depression but the workplace administrators rejected the report. Once the union got involved, he was allowed to remain in his current position until after the trial.

Megan's car only had $300.00 to be paid off, but had to be returned. The DMV would not let Art register the car. Later the Justice Department came after Art because once the car was sold, someone had used it to transport illegal aliens across the border. The car was in Art's name at the time.

On the bright side, Art has a three-month-old baby girl, named Gema.

Art remarked that her name has all the letters of Megan's, except the N. Art told me that an anonymous citizen made a contribution for a chair named in Megan's honor to be placed at the Thousand Oaks Music Center, so symbolically Megan could be present at all the performances.

Susan Barroso was attempting to get on with her life and had completed her degree in Social Work. She gladly shared some photographs of Megan for inclusion in this book, and supports my telling this story.

Josh Reno and Stephen Frueh, former roommates of Sanchez were awarded $10,000 from the city of Moorpark and $25,000 from the city of Simi Valley for the tip that helped to arrest and convict the Simi Valley Rapist.

I have kept in touch with a few of the friends I made on the jury. One of which has reclaimed her teaching position with eighth graders and mother of a precocious six year old. Another male on the jury is still working through his feelings about the case. He does feels that the decision was just and necessary. He states, "If only Sanchez had shown any remorse, it could have gone differently." He and his wife have since moved out of state. Ironically, one of the men had a similar tragedy in his life. He lost his twenty-one year old daughter at the hands of her boyfriend, who later turned the gun on himself. The juror, who had to leave the case before deliberation due to illness, is active with her family, providing childcare and nursing care for her loved-ones. She makes a yearly trip to her grandchildren's school to celebrate "grandmother's day."

As for me, I returned to Youth Authority and continue to teach anger control techniques to troubled teens. My goal is to catch them before they build a lifetime of anger and resentments, and provide them with understanding. Maya

Angelou says, "We do what we know to do. When we learn better, we do better."

Sometimes, in quiet moments I ponder how much of the time most of us spend disconnected from life. I believe that it is because life has gotten so busy, so hectic. We use mindless activities to rest. Do you ever evaluate how few waking hours are spent really getting in touch with how you feel—or what you think about a particular subject?

Pondering life, your life and what it provides you? As a society, we have utilized drugs as one of the most immediate means to disconnect. We manufacture our own escape, instead of finding that quiet place where our mind can rest and reflect.

Being on a death penalty case makes you stop and reflect on what you feel about life. Time to ponder what you are contributing to our world. Will our world be better by having you in it? Will you have made a difference?

I wish to thank many of the people who have made a difference in my world. My husband, Paul for showing patience and support for me while going through this process. The parents of Megan, Susan and Art Barroso for sharing with the world their anguish so the truth could be found. Megan's friends Cricket and Kimberly for their love and support of a dear friend. Crickett's mother, Carol who will be the guardian of Megan's Fund for Cloggers. Kimberly's parents for looking out for her best interest in this trial. Judge Riley for being so very kind and appreciative of us as jurors. The Prosecuting Attorneys and their investigators for their extensive work to seek justice for the Barroso family. The Defense Attorneys and their investigators for giving meaning to the phrase, "justice for all." Both Prosecuting and Defense Attorneys for allowing me to clear my head and add closure to this life-altering event through communication. Dr. Lisa Barra for her insights on survivors' guilt. To A.J., who told it like he felt it! A grand thank you to the sexual assault victims for putting themselves on the line once more to stand and be a voice for all victims of crime.

A special thanks to T.A. Harmon, Carolyn Bishop, June Griffith, Portia Davis and Alicia Valdez for their assistance in editing and polishing this book.

Proceeds from this book will go toward a clogging scholarship called **Megan's Fund.** If you wish to make a contribution, you can do so by mailing to:

Carol Ester
The Fourth Demension (Cloggers)
Megan Barroso Fund
Church of the Nazarene
15518 E. Gale Avenue
Hacienda Heights, California 91745
(626) 968-6811

Judith Ester/Megan Barroso Fund
The Fourth Demension Cloggers
7266 North Jackson Place, Unit A
San Gabriel, California 91775
(818)-625-9195

Printed in the United States
140080LV00001B/3/A